Y0-BZA-118

DECORATING BEGINS WITH YOU

Decorating Begins with You

by MARY JEAN ALEXANDER

Foreword by HAROLD W. GRIEVE
President, American Institute of Decorators

WITH ILLUSTRATIONS

Doubleday & Company, Inc., Garden City, New York 1958

Library of Congress Catalog Card Number 58–12028

Printed in the United States of America
Designed by Diana Klemin
First Edition

Dedicated to

two good friends

Nancy V. McClelland, a great lady

Mildred Irby, an inspired teacher

both of whom helped me to realize that there

is no substitute for knowledge or quality.

ACKNOWLEDGMENTS

With an awareness of help generously given, I would like to express deep appreciation to:

Anne Heywood, who got me started. When she asked me a question and I got on a soap box to answer it, she said, "Why don't you write a book?" So I did.

Mary S. Sproatt, who provided a writing haven during the painful days of early struggle and gave me quantities of faith and encouragement.

Thomas A. Buckley, who helped to select and assemble the period illustrations.

Mildred Mastin Pace, Theodore Adams and Henry Curtis, who gave me constructive professional comment and encouragement.

The nine A.I.D. members who sent me the handsome interiors included—all such convincing evidence of both knowledge and quality.

Sir Hugh Casson, for his prompt and enthusiastic cable.

The Hon. V. Sackville-West, for her friendly co-operation.

The cause of good taste in home decoration is attracting an increasing number of supporters throughout this country and abroad. I would also like to thank the following friends whose active interest and thoughtful questions have encouraged me to write this book:

Mrs. J. W. McCutcheon, Mount Vernon, Iowa; Mrs. John S. Vavra, Cedar Rapids, Iowa; Mrs. Dudley Warner, Livermore, California; Mrs. Ronald Kahler, Atherton, California; Mrs. R. W. Barker, State College, Pennsylvania; Mrs. Paul Trump, Madison, Wisconsin; Mrs. Robert Thiel, Evansville, Indiana; Mrs. Paul Lindig, Decatur, Georgia; Mrs. Charles Findlay, Bronxville, New York; Mrs. Joseph A. Miller, Jr., Cleveland, Ohio; Mrs. F. Curtis Lane, Westfield, Massachusetts; Mrs. John Sproatt, Decorah, Iowa.

And to the authors and publishers for permission to use material from the following:

Calvin S. Hathaway, *Illustrated Survey* of the Museum and *Chronicle*, Vol. 2, No. 9, August 1957.

Sir Hugh Casson, *Improvements—The New Yorker*, June 1, 1957.

Frank Lloyd Wright, *Genius and the Mobocracy*, Duell, Sloan and Pierce, copyright 1949.

Philip C. Johnson, *Mies Van der Rohe*, Museum of Modern Art, copyright 1947.

Frederick Mortimer Clapp, *Cadenza in C Minor*, The Spiral Press, Inc., copyright 1957.

Henry-Russell Hitchcock, *Built in U.S.A., Post War Architecture*, Museum of Modern Art, copyright March 1952.

Emily Genauer, review of exhibition of Antoni Gaudi at Museum of Modern Art in *Herald Tribune*, December 22, 1957.

V. Sackville-West, *Knole and the Sackvilles*, Ernest Benn.

Bernard Berenson, *Seeing and Knowing*, Chapman and Hall, Ltd., The Macmillan Company, copyright January 1954.

John E. Burchard and Albert Bush-Brown, "The Architect, More Needed than Pitied"—*Harper's Magazine*, May 1957.

John Maass, *The Gingerbread Age*, Rinehart and Company, copyright 1957.

William Pahlmann, *The Pahlmann Book of Interior Design*, Thomas Y. Crowell Company, copyright 1955.

FOREWORD

It is becoming increasingly evident that in order to have the practical and well-co-ordinated home of today, a certain amount of special knowledge is necessary.

Through the reading of *Decorating Begins with You*, you can add to your store of knowledge. This book explains the numerous details which are a part of interior designing, such as scale, proportion, arrangement, buying, and color. It brings to the attention of the reader the unlimited number of arts and crafts that should be understood and, in turn fused, to create a well-balanced home.

Although there may be a waning interest in the true period room, it is still desirable to have a speaking acquaintance with the past. In any project, one must start at the beginning and work steadily onward, profiting from retrospection and past cultures.

Background has a prevailing influence in our daily existence. It should be a counterpart of our personality and it takes a well-informed person with a workable training in the arts of interior design to accomplish this.

Much valuable and sound advice is presented in this book. It is not reading for a rainy afternoon. It is serious and should be a must on the list of anyone who intends to take an active part in the decoration of his home. Mrs. Alexander brings to the attention of the reader as much knowledge as is possible in a limited space, and this book will further stimulate interest in decoration and the correlated arts. The sincere desire of the writer is to improve the art of interior design and decoration.

The interior designer should be constantly searching for ways to use the new materials which science keeps developing and the abundance of new items which flood the markets each year. For instance, the Thermopane window now makes the large glass areas of the Southwest also practical in less tropical climates. There are no limitations to what can be done in the world of design today.

The last hundred years have pushed aside structural barriers and the new concept of architecture has made the planning of interiors more of a challenge than ever before.

The simple and straightforward manner of Mrs. Alexander's book has great value for the homemaker who wants to understand and co-operate with a decorator. It is equally useful for the "do-it-yourself" homemaker; and also the material is an important source of information for the student of design and decoration. It will stimulate the desire to ever continue the pursuit of the perpetually improving modern home.

Harold W. Grieve
President, American Institute of Decorators

CONTENTS

Foreword 9

Introduction 19

1 YOU HAVE TASTE—DEVELOP CONFIDENCE IN IT 25

You have taste. This implies the ability to choose. Make your taste an enlightened one on the basis of sound principles. How you can translate your personal likes and dislikes into understandable taste trends.

2 NUTSHELL GUIDE TO GOOD DECORATING 39

Where to start in organizing your project. Importance of budget and floor plan at the beginning. Practical discussion of function, explanation of unity, scale, proportion, line, and form as they apply to the interior.

ILLUSTRATIONS

Key to credits beneath halftone illustrations: *Met*—Courtesy of the Metropolitan Museum of Art; *CU*—Courtesy, Cooper Union Museum; *Fr.*—Courtesy, French and Co.

COLOR ILLUSTRATIONS

INTRODUCTION

Since I was first exposed to the French language, during my college days, I have never stopped trying to speak it—with remarkable lack of success. Periodically I pursue it by attending a class and recently I audited a course at a Midwestern college. My speech failed to show any noticeable improvement, but I did get something from the course. I learned a phrase which is well-known to any Francophile and it has stayed with me: "*Chacun à son goût*"—each to his own taste. I have found myself using it so frequently that I decided to observe just how and why, and the answer to both was very simple. Too many people are too commonly telling too many other people how to think—and to live.

As a decorator, I read many articles in the field of design and I have become increasingly aware of the fact that in this field as in most others this useful French suggestion is almost completely ignored. There is, today, an unbelievable amount of "expert" advice and taste being pressed on the public. I have come to the conclusion that someone should, in a calm, sensible, and reasonable way, remind you that this will always be with us; and we need not be unduly swayed by it, nor unduly confused by its contradictions. I hope to give you some practical suggestions that can guide you through this superabundance of advice, and at the same time help you gain confidence in your own taste.

The quantity of writing in the field has increased so much in the past decade that it would require a library to hold any one part of it. This material is in the form of books, magazine articles, which increase rapidly because of their monthly publication, and newspapers—especially Sunday supplement sections. And all this in addition to the advertising. There has also been a great deal said in lectures and all kinds of informal talks, much of which is eventually published. It would be impossible to read one tenth of this, even if one wanted to, but it has seemed to me that a sort of preliminary short course would benefit what one does read, and help toward a better understanding and evaluation, on a personal basis. Interior design has a rather special terminology, and a glossary that you may find useful in clarifying the meanings of words you will run across in the writing on this subject will be found at the end of the book.

The many references to names of people and particular places assume a general knowledge and a specific kind of information that many of us do not have. Such a term as Bauhaus has had meaning for me—but if anyone had asked me to explain it fully, I would have stuttered a few generalities. When I mentioned it recently to a friend who is both intelligent and interested in certain phases of design, she thought it was a religion. Mies Van der Rohe is often called simply Mies, much to the confusion of people who may be interested but who have only a vague understanding. Even his full name, and also the name Corbusier, have rung a rather faint bell. Organic design is a very specific thing but it had a hazy connotation for me, mainly because it has also been discussed so much more frequently than explained.

In addition, there is the ever-present and damnably convincing controversial material. It CAN'T all be true, but in order to know where you stand it is necessary to get an angle on both sides of a controversy—unless it is your own, in which case you already have your angle. I believe that if you can steer through the fog created by this vast volume of writing—much of which is opinionated—you will find quantities of good literature and learn to judge the good designers not on the period or style they represent but purely on the basis of their net contribution. The antagonism between the extreme conservatives and the intolerant moderns has caused a vast amount of confusion, but it is possible to find both intelligent traditionalists and tolerant moderns, if you look. There has been much criticism, both fair and unfair, objective and personal, and some of those criticized have replied. No matter how radical some may be and whether or not you agree with them, many are sincere.

Quality and personal preference should be the basis of judgment for the average person who dips into this literature because he is interested in having a better home. So much ridicule has been directed toward traditionalists by ardent modernists and so much scorn returned to them by the traditionalists that the public has been led to believe that the choice must be between the two—traditional or modern. This should be second to quality and preference. The case is one for good design, without regard to kind of style and with heavy emphasis on suitability at a completely personal level. It should be good, it should have taste—but equally important—it should be right for the people who are to live in it. It is essential that you acquire the knowledge necessary to make your choice a right and intelligent one for YOU.

The process requires genuine interest and an open mind. We are all vaguely familiar with the design of the past, but much of the modern design is startlingly new. In order to like it, usually you must first understand it. I have learned to enjoy a great deal of modern music and painting by listening and looking and trying to understand it; in doing so I have added to my own aesthetic resources. After majoring in Political Science in college, I got involved with art for the first time, opening a whole new world. But that did not lessen my interest in politics or in history, which has continued to be another source of contact. This switch of interest has proved to me that any subject you care enough about to cultivate can add not only to your knowledge and understanding but to your confidence and discrimination. It can be a superb antidote for overspecialization; and through learning to appreciate and enjoy over a broader range, your life will truly be enriched.

In the domain of art—of which design is such an important part—I would like to pose this question. What is an artist? When I went back to school to study interior design I became fascinated with the business of perspective, along with drawing and painting. Many times, when I have been struggling to get my impression of some subject that appeals to me on a piece of painting paper,

I have had someone stop by me and ask, "Are you an artist?" I've never known what to answer. Obviously these people—sometimes children, often not—consider an artist a person who paints or draws on paper or canvas. I've been thinking about it for years and although I'm sure it has been discussed and properly defined, I firmly believe that anyone who has the capacity to appreciate and accept beauty in a way that enriches his life is something of an artist. But it must be genuine and honest or none of it is worth a tinker's damn. Are you an artist? Think it over before you deny it.

Men are sharing more and more of the activities of the home and this book is addressed not only to the women who are the backbone of the domestic scene, but to any man who cares, whether or not he is especially active. Any person, male or female, who is interested in some phase of the general subject of design as applied to the home can acquire a basic familiarity with it from this book. It is planned to awaken and develop taste, increase discrimination and confidence, arouse imagination, and stimulate and encourage any latent creative ability you may have for the making or improving of your home. It is intended, in a sincere, simple, and sensible way, to help *you* have what *you* want in your home—with taste and in good design.

DECORATING BEGINS WITH YOU

1

You Have Taste—Develop Confidence in It

Whether you believe it or not—and whether you like it or not—you have taste. You may prefer chocolate ice cream to vanilla, a vacation at the seashore to one in the mountains, or fluffy ruffles to severe pleats—and everyone has a favorite color. So you do have taste, but have you confidence in it? Perhaps THEY aren't using ruffles this year, or it is much more chic to be seen at Estes Park than Cape Cod or Martha's Vineyard. Or, you just don't DO a room with yellow (your favorite color). Would this pressure affect your feelings about any of these? There seems to be in progress a concentrated, persistent, and efficacious conspiracy devised to weaken your confidence in your own taste.

What do we know about taste? It is a tricky business and I have never seen a satisfactory definition of it. Mr. Webster calls it a nice perception of artistic excellence, which gives us a clue. A thoughtful friend has very aptly described it as enlightened choice, and in our field it certainly implies the ability to choose on the basis of sound principles of design. But even though it can't be defined exactly, there are many things we know about it. As one studies good art or design and gradually realizes just what makes them good, his taste develops and he becomes understanding of and sensitive to an increasing number of combinations of design and color. As he gradually learns to appreciate the more subtle of these, his standards improve. This improvement is of the cumulative kind and becomes a part of his experience. Calvin S. Hathaway, director of the Cooper Union Museum, has said, "If truth is constant, human perception is less so; the eye is not an entirely objective agent, and all too often it sees only what it is told to look for. Of such discrepancies in vision, comparable to changes in barometric pressure, is composed the history of taste." It is further complicated by being a somewhat local quality. As anyone knows who has traveled at all, what is considered good in one part of the world may be completely unappreciated in another. Fortunately for our purpose this applies less to design than to any other cultural area.

Taste is not a constant aspect and while only a small number of people are born with instinctive good taste, everyone is born with some. There are very few people who cannot progress from a status of actually poor taste to one of sound good taste—if they are interested enough to make a sincere effort. Flair is not to be confused with taste. One must be born with flair and it may have a slightly giddy quality which can quickly turn into bad taste if it isn't controlled. Taste, in itself, is not as creative as flair at its best, but it can be developed by anyone who is conscious of its existence and who has a strong enough desire to do so.

It can be roughly divided into categories: flawless, good, fair or passable and poor or bad. Flawless or actual bad taste is scarcely subject to opinion. One is so fine that there can be little question of its quality and the other is so bad that no opinion can accept it as good. On these two levels it is almost a science and any jury would be apt to agree. People with flawless taste need no help and those with truly bad taste are unlikely to have enough consciousness of it to realize what they are missing. Between these two poles there is room for a variety of personal opinion—likes and dislikes—and that is as it should be. It is within this bracket that we find the many homeowners whose confidence has been so weakened by the conspiracy mentioned.

During the past few years, in the field of interior design and decoration, there has been an immeasurable amount of promotion circulated. It has been done through the advertising of furniture, fabrics, wall and floor coverings and accessories, through public relations experts working diligently, and through the home magazines. In accepting this, the consumer has unconsciously permitted himself to be led down all kinds of garden paths, few of which end up anywhere. The quantity of resourceful and competent material presented in such dizzying volume is comparable to a *smörgåsbord* where you are given a quick once-around whirl and expected to know just what you want for dinner.

The result is an inevitable confusion which not only breaks down what confidence you may have been carefully building up, but makes you fearful of admitting publicly to liking or disliking anything (unless you hear some allegedly official acceptance or refusal). There are unquestionably many wonderful things to be had—and for you—from this fabulous market. But first you should build up the courage to follow the maxim "to thine own self be true." In order to combat the confusion resulting from the constant overdose of rich, colorful, and adroitly tempting display, you will have to arrive at some definite views of your own. It is unlikely that you will find the necessary courage unless you do.

To accomplish this, sit down and list, as comprehensively as you can, what you most emphatically do and don't like in reference to your way of living, or the way you would choose to live. This should include function, appearance, and personal whims of all kinds. Don't be vague or obscure in your mustering of your opinions; be specific. At the back of the book there are pages provided where you can start your notations. Next, make a scrapbook. No time is too soon to start collecting photos or sketches, from any source at all, that appeal to you. One of the substantial advantages of this practice is that you have them where you can refer to them easily and visually whenever you wish. Consequently you don't forget them and if you need to explain them to anyone, one picture is better than ten minutes of description. Then, as you analyze some of your favorite schemes, make an effort to understand the trend of your taste. Why do they please you? What do they have in common? There may be a variety of answers to both questions, but if you keep at it, certain consistent qualities will emerge. Sort them through carefully, a few at a time, and try to perceive what it is that you find most satisfactory in each. Your personal whims are bound to be at the bottom of your taste. Keep it personal. Don't ever discourage your instinctive inclinations until you have tried them out. Give them a chance.

It has been said that the cultured man is not vague, that what he does know he is definite about, and in addition he has a keen awareness of what he doesn't know. There has been too much vagueness in the field of design—too much discussion of and reference to subjects and names that are not often or clearly enough defined. I hope this book will contribute to culture by helping you to clarify your own ideas and consequently overcome any tendency to vagueness that you may have. That is the purpose of the check list or test that has been worked out, and if you make the effort, you can accomplish a little cultural job for yourself at the same time you are figuring out exactly what kind of tastes you have.

Now you are ready for the test which follows. It is designed to help you understand and, through understanding, to discover, the kind of background particularly suited to YOU—the one that will be the best and psychologically most sympathetic. It is a new kind of test and not akin to the many tests that are merely a weighing of your taste against that of someone trained in the field—a somewhat arbitrary procedure. It will help you to realize what type of background should make you feel happiest and best adjusted.

You are more interested in your ideas than in those of anyone else—understandably and naturally. You want to do something—but do you know what you want? This is where you must be careful to hang on for dear life to your own identity and find out for yourself just what it is that you do want. You have the right to express whatever you like, but if you show signs of indecision you will probably find yourself, and promptly, the victim of someone who has sufficient confidence for both of you—but who does not have YOUR taste. There can never be a pat formula for planning a right home that is valid for everyone, but in spite of that incontestable fact, too many people ask for it and they can always find someone willing to offer it.

You will need a little background—of simple fundamentals, color, and a brief discussion of respective virtues and disadvantages of modern and traditional design. This follows in the next chapters. The test is planned to give you a scientific hand in understanding what kind of a home can best contribute to your happiness. If you are scrupulously honest in taking the test (you can't kid a test) and read the book thoughtfully, you will soon feel your presently deflated but basically sound self-confidence stealing back into your consciousness. Welcome it with emphatic recognition, and then relax and feel free to tell *anyone* what you do and don't like.

WHAT TYPE OF HOME FOR ME?

This check-list test can be fun—stimulating and helpful.

It will aid in focusing your attention on the variety of influences to be considered when you plan your new home or consider any decorating problem. You can score the test yourself with a blank sheet of paper and a pencil, and it will be interesting to compare your results with those of your friends—and to discuss possible reasons for their being alike or different. Get a blank sheet of paper and a pencil ready and go ahead. There is no time limit.

PART I Things you like to do In each group of five statements, choose the *two* things that you would like most to do. Choose *two*, but only two statements, from each group. Make *two* choices even if it may seem difficult to in some instances. When you have chosen a statement, put its number on your blank piece of paper—this will be used later in scoring.

1 Go to a Parent-Teachers' committee meeting
2 Attend a neighborhood movie
3 Attend a church service
4 Go to a home-furnishings exhibit
5 Listen to a lecture on the international situation

6 Read the local-society section of a newspaper
7 Read the editorial section of a newspaper
8 Read the sports section of a newspaper
9 Read the local news in a newspaper
10 Read the household-hints section of a newspaper

11 Shop for a spring hat
12 Browse through old stores for antiques
13 Shop for dresser-scarf sets
14 Shop for inexpensive secondhand chairs
15 Shop for a beautiful but simple oriental scroll

16 Work in your garden
17 Rummage through old boxes in the attic
18 Plan a dinner for a family or friends
19 Write letters to relatives in other cities
20 Write an article or commentary for a professional journal

21 Select the materials for making some new curtains
22 Make the curtains according to your taste, and hang them
23 Explain to others how curtains are selected, made, and hung
24 Show friends the room in which your new curtains are of central interest
25 Find the best possible decorator to handle curtain problems

PART II Things you like or don't like Again, choose *two* statements out of each group of five. Select the *two* things you like best of those listed within the group (even if you don't really like any of them, or like them all). Be sure to choose *two,* but not more than two, from each block of five. Record your selections by number, just as you did for Part I.

26 Admiration from your friends
27 Loyalty from your friends
28 Affection from your friends
29 Respect from your friends
30 Attention from your friends

31 Picnics
32 Cocktail parties
33 Cafeteria meals
34 Tearoom luncheons
35 Buffet dinners

36 Mathematics
37 Literature
38 Dramatics
39 Social psychology
40 Applied sciences

41 Optimists
42 Polite people
43 Witty people
44 Logical people
45 Thrifty, practical people

46 A job with a respectable-sounding title
47 Steady employment
48 Congenial personal relations on the job
49 Opportunity to try out your ideas
50 Variety in the work to avoid monotony

PART III *Choose the* two *statements,* in each group of five, that you feel describe yourself best. Choose the *two* best from each group whether or not you feel they really describe you accurately. The over-all pattern of answers is what counts, not a particular individual case. But don't skip any, or your score will suffer. Make the best choices you can and record them, as before.

51 A good mixer socially
52 Thorough in every detail
53 Completely reliable
54 Quite aggressive
55 Always natural and at ease

56 Have a great many friends
57 Have few, but close, friends
58 Inclined to be quiet and a little self-effacing
59 Make friends casually under almost any conditions
60 Enjoy and depend, to some extent, on the attention of others

61 Like to argue, but even-tempered
62 Quite conciliatory in most situations
63 Enjoy being different from the run of the mill
64 Go along with the crowd if personal matters are not involved
65 Make every effort to avoid or forestall disputes

66 Quite precise about details
67 Leave details to others whenever possible
68 Very good at conceiving and developing plans
69 Best at administering plans already established
70 Like to "plan as you go along"

71 Good at looking at problems from every possible viewpoint
72 Good at adapting old ideas or materials to new uses
73 Good at thinking up unusual and new ideas quickly
74 Good at spotting defects or deficiencies in daily situations
75 Good at breaking away completely from habitual thinking

76 Are objective and open-minded
77 Have strong opinions and are not afraid to back them up
78 Enjoy telling jokes to groups of people
79 Like to play around with ideas, especially novel ones
80 Do not care much about other people's opinions about yourself

81 Like to talk with two or three people with similar interests
82 Enjoy being a part of a fairly large social group
83 Like private chats with influential persons
84 Like to chat with old friends, one at a time
85 Enjoy talking to anybody, if he is not pressed for time

86 Like to live in the city, particularly New York
87 Prefer the characteristics of suburban life
88 Like to be isolated from noise, people, centers of activity
89 Restlessness urges change of location every few years
90 Like "elbow room" even if the place may be a bit run down

91 Foreigners stimulate and enrich your life
92 Distrustful of "foreigners" though perhaps you like some
93 Find it almost impossible to answer an ambiguous question
94 Have no trouble at all answering ambiguous questions
95 Consider possible results before deciding questions of ethics

96 Take life very seriously, regret that others don't do so more
97 Take life lightly, a day at a time
98 Prefer to be a big frog in a little pond
99 Would rather be a little frog in a big pond
100 Look on life as an experiment—no one knows the answer

101 Outwardly a good loser, but it rankles for a long time inside
102 A hard loser in every respect—and show it
103 Easy come, easy go—a good loser with no grudges
104 Act like a poor loser at the time, but really accept it philosophically
105 Very unemotional—act and feel almost the same whether you win or lose

106 Consider most people, "the mass," rather stupid
107 Consider almost everyone, saint or sinner, basically good
108 Consider all but close friends potentially, if not actually, suspicious
109 Accept everyone as a good person until proved wrong
110 Consider only people with colorful personalities as "worthwhile"

111 Believe in an actual physical Hell in the hereafter
112 Think most people should believe in Hell for their own good
113 Consider Hell a superstition carried over from the old days
114 Feel that actually everybody will really go to Heaven
115 Do not care whether there is a Hell or not

116 Are tactful out of an inner sense of kindness
117 Want to be tactful, but in being earnest, sometimes lose tact
118 Tact is an instrument—to be used where it will do the most good
119 Feel honesty comes before tact, except in special situations
120 Kindly—but rarely conscious of the concept of tact

121 Thin-skinned; feelings are fairly easily hurt
122 Thick-skinned; not bothered by what others say about you
123 Become flustered when under observation or supervision
124 Like sharing rewards and responsibility as member of a "team"
125 Accept supervision only if the supervisor is a qualified superior

SCORING INSTRUCTIONS FOR THE TEST

What Type of Home for Me? The scoring is based on five TYPES of homes. Each choice you made in the test counts one point for one or another of the types. Below are the home types with a brief description of each—and the test answers that count for that particular type. Your score can easily be added up by counting the responses you made which are counted for Type A, B, C,

D, or E. It is fun to have several friends take the test and compare scores—then discuss why your scores are similar or different.

TYPE A—Contemporary Conventional This type of home is best exemplified by the average real estate dealer's offering in a city or suburban development. House is usually pretty new, though it may need some repairs. Designed for efficient modern life, although rooms are likely to be small and boxlike compared with older houses. Many electrical gadgets to reduce the drudgery of household chores. Often comparatively new materials will have been used. Ceilings likely to be low, and little space between your house and your neighbors'. You may be able to mutually "enjoy" each other's Hi-Fi and TV sets. It is a fairly standard American home—clean, convenient—but not inspiring in spirit.

SCORING POINTS 1, 9, 11, 18, 24, 26, 31, 39, 41, 46, 54, 56, 64, 69, 71, 78, 83, 87, 95, 99, 101, 107, 112, 118, 124.

TYPE B—Old-Fashioned Usually found in smaller towns, or in the older sections of a city. Likely to be rather small in terms of number of rooms, but the rooms may be more spacious than in Type A, the ceilings higher, and there may be both an attic and cellar. Antiques and heirlooms may dominate the furnishings. There is likely to be a piano, and perhaps no TV. There will be a tendency toward fussiness and ornamentation in furnishings. Pictures will be reproductions of old artists of the schools of Rosa Bonheur or Landseer. Doilies, bric-a-brac, and quaint pieces of furniture will give the home a quiet charm, but one not too intimately geared to the demands of modern life.

SCORING POINTS 3, 6, 13, 19, 22, 27, 34, 37, 42, 48, 53, 58, 65, 66, 74, 77, 84, 88, 92, 96, 102, 108, 111, 116, 121.

TYPE C—Modernistic, Sophisticated Severe, chic, efficient—a minimum of ornamentation, and a maximum of built-in gadgets. An emphasis on efficiency and expensive elegance. Much glass used to bring in direct light from outside. Ingenious use of concealed artificial light. Straight lines and smooth sleek surfaces predominate. Objects of oriental origin often used for decoration. Interior itself may reflect a strong oriental influence. Severe, sophisticated, and often charming.

SCORING POINTS 5, 7, 15, 20, 25, 29, 35, 36, 44, 49, 52, 57, 61, 68, 75, 76, 81, 86, 93, 100, 105, 106, 113, 119, 125.

TYPE D—"Barn into a House" This house gives maximum expression to owner's personality. House may be actually or figuratively made from a barn. Many old objects have been converted to uses entirely unrelated to their previous functions (i.e., a spinning wheel made over into a floor lamp). Extensive use often made of bargain materials, used originally. House usually in a state of change and alteration. Represents creative activity—highly personalized.

SCORING POINTS 4, 10, 12, 17, 21, 30, 32, 38, 43, 50, 51, 60, 63, 70, 72, 79, 82, 89, 91, 98, 104, 110, 115, 117, 123.

TYPE E—"House into a Barn" This type of house is large, amorphous, and follows no set style or design—although at one time it may have. Occupant is one who wants room and freedom from restrictions and social pressures of all kinds. House may have been an old mansion in a currently unfashionable part of town—now repaired and functional, more so than ever before. Very little reflection of the occupant's personality except for its practicalness and haphazard style. Has an air of informality—nothing done for the impression it will make. A good place to work, rest, and pursue special interests. Maximum of space, minimum of planning and care.

SCORING POINTS 2, 8, 14, 16, 23, 28, 33, 40, 45, 47, 55, 59, 62, 67, 73, 80, 85, 90, 94, 97, 103, 109, 114, 120, 122.

When you have added up the total number of points "earned" for each of the above five types, you will be able to evaluate your test in this way:

21 or more points	A definite compatability between your personality and interest pattern and the type of home indicated. Spend a good bit of time investigating these possibilities further in the light of your own situation.
16 to 20 points	This type of home should receive serious consideration too. But keep a wary eye open for characteristics in the house that might not quite suit you.
11 to 15 points	This type of home has both advantages and disadvantages about evenly balanced for you.
6 to 10 points	There seem to be substantial elements in your interest and personality patterns that do not fit this type of home very well. If this does not seem to agree with your personal feelings, check into the situation carefully.
0 to 5 points	Such a wide discrepancy between your personality and interest patterns and those that appear to be suited to this type of house suggests that you spend most of your time and effort considering types of houses on which you made higher scores.

2

Nutshell Guide to Good Decorating

Every human being who loves a home deserves to have one that satisfies him; one in which all members of the family can be comfortable, can carry on their own individual activities without getting in each other's hair, and in which they can experience the satisfaction and pleasure of sympathetic surroundings. Your home must be functional and that is the first requisite—but it is a means to a larger end and not the end. And of course it must operate for all members of the family. Beyond that, the home should be a haven for each member, and whether or not they know or understand it, this is where the aesthetic becomes practical.

Mrs. L., a client, lived in a large house, bought mainly because it was available. She didn't exactly hate the house but it was impossible to make of it the kind of home she wanted. As a result of frustration, she became what was locally known as "run down." She found her temper short, which made her cross with herself, and her housework never seemed to give her any satisfaction. When conditions permitted, she and her husband built a house to suit them both. A great deal of time and thought and as much money as possible was spent on the furnishings, and I was called in as decorator. Recognizing the problem, I went all-out in an effort to satisfy the personal likes of Mrs. L.—within the bounds of good taste. Today Mrs. L. is a different person. Everything she does in her new house gives her satisfaction and she feels fine and full of energy for what used to be the daily grind. Sometimes, in the middle of her work, she stops and just sits down and luxuriates in the pleasures of her home. She may drop down on the sofa in the living room and enjoy the colors, or the sight of an especially beautiful lamp within range. She may go into her bedroom, where an entirely different color scheme satisfies her equally. But wherever she goes she relaxes and this atmosphere that has been created for her has proved beneficial in a very practical way.

A good and well-trained interior decorator can always be helpful, as discussed in Chapter 4. But for the many situations where work of this kind needs to be done and no decorating service is available, as well as for those persons who would like to understand more about the basic rules that govern design—frequently abstruse in its implications—this chapter provides a nutshell guide to decorating. Good design is timeless, so the fundamental principles are unchanging. The following applies to any good style of furniture or architecture, from Early American, through eighteenth-century, French or English, to any variety of modern.

Where should you start? It is always wise to start with your floor plan. The magazines have been very generous with good ones and if you are building, it is often possible to find the kind of thing you want, which you can have adjusted to your own specific use. You may also find practical suggestions if you are remodeling, but in either case you will end up with a better house for less money if you call in a good and reputable architect. Today's architect must be an engineer, and with the thousands of running feet of space required for your heating, wiring, plumbing, etc., you will certainly get what you want in the safest and most economical way by hiring a specialist. This is definitely a job for a professional and even the best contractor can't work it out for your maximum convenience as well or as economically as an architect.

The first thing to do is analyze the layout of your house or apartment with regard to the function of each room in its relationship to adjoining rooms. There are a number of items to be checked in this connection. As far as is practical, let the rooms that will be used most during sunny hours be on the sunny side. Rooms that call for special privacy should be at the end of a hall when possible, to avoid the noise of passing traffic. Avoid having rooms where people will be up late talking, playing music, or listening to the "Late Late Show" next to a room where the baby—or anyone else in the family—likes to go to bed early. Utilize your space so that it can be the most effective for the good of all. Don't, as some friends of mine did, either set aside a large room for someone who will seldom be in it, or count on apparently temporary setups remaining temporary. Mr. and Mrs. J., whose children had left home, were approached by a distant cousin who planned to take a job in their town, asking if she might stay with them while looking for a permanent residence. The J.s had recently moved into a small house with only one large bedroom besides their own, and a small sewing room with a studio couch. With the idea that she would be there a few weeks at the longest, they turned over to Cousin H. the very attractive second bedroom. She found the room, with its connecting bath, much more comfortable and infinitely more economical than anything she could locate and she stayed on. Her work kept her out all day and frequently in the evenings. When the J.s' daughter came home, having arranged for work locally that she would do free lance, from the home, they made the mistake of putting her into the sewing room. The complications that were involved in the resolution of the situation were hectic and caused hard feelings all around. Even though the J.s didn't expect their guest to become a permanent resident, they knew that she would rarely be at home and they would have been much wiser if they had moved the sewing things into the large bedroom and given her the small room. Although unexpected situations will arise, try to work out the arrangement that best fits the needs of the most members of the family and makes for the smoothest operation.

One of your major concerns is function. If you have the room and the furniture, experiment with placing it where it seems to best fulfill its purpose. If the rooms are not yet in existence, draw a floor plan at ¼-inch scale. You will certainly have the dimensions of your rooms, so measure them out, letting ¼ of an inch equal 1 foot and showing all openings, both windows and doors. Measure each piece of furniture—width and length—and place the measurements on a piece of brown wrapping paper. Cut them out so you can move them around on your floor plan, knowing that they will fill the same space on your plan that they will in the room. If your furniture is not available—hasn't been bought or is in storage—you can estimate sizes with sufficient accuracy by measuring similar pieces and estimating the size of your own. This floor plan is a good start but it is not conclusive. It shows you exactly the space each piece will displace, but it tells you nothing about how it will look where you have placed it. And that is absolutely essential, because in the total effect the arrangement of the furniture is second only to color in importance. And bear in mind, *always,* that you should aim to place every object in the room so that it accomplishes its purpose in the most effective manner.

A few general rules should be remembered. Keep your rooms sufficiently open so that passage through is clear—including the way to windows that must be opened or closed. The more important pieces of furniture should not interfere with the architectural features or compete with them in any way. Try to balance them. A tall secretary beside a door, opposite a wall where only low furniture is used, will make a badly balanced room. Every piece should be easily available for its particular function. None should be out of scale with the room—no heavy pieces in small rooms, and small ones used in large rooms should be grouped so as not to appear lost. Avoid putting too much furniture in one part of the room, leaving another part empty, even if you have to do some juggling to keep the function intact. Never crowd a room; a room with too much furniture will never be restful and it will make people instinctively uncomfortable. Generally, furniture and rugs placed with the lines of the room rather than against give a better feeling of harmony.

Most people today, and especially those who are raising families, work with a budget. You may not be able to figure closely at this point, but this is where your budget should start, and unless you have one you are more than likely to end up with a very spotty house. Guard against becoming too interested in kitchen equipment; it is easy to get carried away and allow yourself to be sold on much more than your budget permits. Saying to your spouse, "This is for a long time and is actually an economy," you may run out of money before the house is furnished. I know a case where just that happened and the family ended up with the cheapest kind of upholstered furniture and beds, all of which had to be replaced. If they had stayed carefully within a budget and waited until later for some of the expensive kitchen appliances, allowing adequate space in their original plan, they would have been operating on a much sounder basis. So do start with a budget and stay within it after you have it. Let it be an over-all one at first, and then, as you know more definitely about your plans, break it down accurately.

You are ready now to get out your scrapbook. Every idea that appeals to you and all illustrations of interiors that you have liked should be here. Spend lots of time mulling over this collection until you feel that all interested parties, which usually includes any members of the family able to talk, have had some kind of a meeting of minds. Be unequivocally sensible in your first plan and restrain a very human tendency to be arbitrary or emotional about it. A top magazine editor who has her finger close to the pulse of the American woman has told me that it is a fact that there are two things wanted (and usually gotten) more than anything else for the home: a large and "good" sofa—no economizing here—and wall-to-wall carpeting. If you have this urge, don't indulge it until it makes sense in your general plan. One young lady who had set the date for her wedding went into business by purchasing a very expensive eight-foot sofa. If you have the money (she didn't really), that is simple. But what then? In the city, where she lived, how many apartments can accommodate such a piece of furniture? Very few, as she soon discovered, and the same is true of most of the smaller houses. When she did find the apartment she had to take it at the sacrifice of other desirable essentials, and moving the sofa in was a major project, requiring a special hoist, removal of windows, and all kinds of extra trouble and expense. The sofa simply was not worth it and she fully realized it by that time. Very recently, a decorating editor who had been covering the Chicago furniture market announced to me that her information indicated that young people usually still buy their sofa first, but just as another piece, and not as their one really extravagant purchase. If this is the trend, it sounds like a step in the right direction.

In your original planning, include all of the things that you hope to have to make it the home you want. Then classify the list either by eliminating the least important or listing the most essential. A very practical method is to list everything on a graded scale and then start with the essentials—but with an eye always on your overall scheme. You will produce a much more satisfactory home, using this method, with a minimum of precious funds spent on objects which really don't belong and ultimately will be discarded. This also enables you to start seeing results much sooner than you possibly can with haphazard buying and this process is cumulative. The visual progress will be more encouraging than all the talk and dreams in the world.

The first and most important requisite of any selection is your own personal reaction to it. This is your home and you not only must like it but should let it reflect your own personality. While this takes precedence, you must not let it obstruct function, comfort, or successful decorative effect. Make your selections thoughtfully and have a practical and definite reason for every choice. Frank Alvah Parsons, one of the first people to promote interior design as a profession and as one that required special training, started a school, now called Parsons School of Design—also the first —for this purpose. He used to compare the assembling and decorating of a room with the building of a word in a word game. Choosing S I M P L E, as his example, in terms of your room, he said that you should buy the article that supplies the missing letter, and when the letters are all there—stop. Any object, no matter how beautiful or how good a bargain, that is not part of your original plan is superfluous. This may seem a rather inflexible rule and, taken too literally, could be. But in a general way it implies some very good advice. Too little is better than too much and emphatically so at the beginning. So do restrain your impulse to do a lot of decorating and just aim to be sure that everything is both suitable to its purpose and satisfactory in appearance, in a very simple way. Sincerity is necessary and affectation will ruin the real quality. If you do it this way, from repeated right experience, you will develop knowledge and understanding—and consequently improve your taste.

Within your own experience, attempt to maintain a high standard of taste. Anything that involves correctness for its own sake will most certainly give a self-conscious effect that won't fool anyone, so watch out for that. If you like living casually, let your home be casual, with character, and don't let it turn into a dumping ground.

You are, at this point, embarking on a major project and, don't forget—this is a *beginning*. Your home will be growing. Start with a house or apartment that is simple and natural, and let it have a chance to grow with you. Your taste will develop and change and the fewer early mistakes, where you have indulged some questionable urge (possibly to impress), the less it will be necessary to discard as your home gradually evolves into the background you want.

Any room that is to be harmonious must have unity. The best definition and the most expressive one that I have ever heard is Leonardo da Vinci's, "Every part is disposed to unite with the whole that it may thereby escape its own incompleteness." In a room this means that each object must maintain its own identity and at the same time contribute to the total effect. In household language it involves the combination of furniture, wall and floor treatment, accessories and color which have something in common in appearance and purpose. Each depends on the others and in an orderly way creates the whole. The drawing on the following page illustrates a room that is lacking in harmony. Your eye can't possibly take in so much scattered pattern and keeps jumping around. Following page 120 is another picture of the same room. The ugly window (which was also useless), the distracting panels, and the unsightly table legs have disappeared. The curtains, hung from the cornice (can be taken down easily for cleaning), cover the wall and make a background for paintings and a mirror, which add to the interest, character, and design of the room. Without changing the furniture and simply by eliminating the disrupting lines made by the badly designed architecture, the composition has been pulled together and

in the process the room has acquired simplicity and a quiet unity.

This is a concrete example of working with an existing situation to achieve harmony in a single room and each room should have its own unity. The entire house or apartment should also be conceived of as a unit, the rooms blending together to make the larger but equally harmonious whole. With the variety of personalities represented in many families, there must also be some variety of style, but it isn't necessary for one room to be so violently different that it destroys the general peaceful effect. In this connection, beware of persuasive advertising and especially if it includes anything not in your sensible plan, or is promoting some new fashion trend. This kind of buying is very likely not only to date your room but to interfere with or even defy the feeling of harmony you are striving for.

Scale and proportion, both relative qualities, may seem difficult to separate. Don't try, because it is easier to understand them together. Scale is the relation of each part of an object to another part and to the whole. Actually, scale means the size of anything in comparison to what you are used to. Everything seems large or small by comparison or contrast with the other objects in a room; the idea is to keep the sizes and shapes of all furniture and spaces nicely related. Good scale requires that all parts of an object must be related in a satisfying way—not only to each other, but to the object, everything else in the room, and the room itself. Proportion means the shape of one area in relation to the whole that contains it. The proportions of a chair are good if the dimensions—height, depth, width—are harmonious. The proportion of a room is good if the windows and doors seem right within their walls and if the wall dimensions are agreeable. Good proportion, in general, requires all sizes, forms, and shapes to be pleasingly related. This can refer to the relationship of a picture to its mat and frame, of the framed picture to its wall space, or a large piece of furniture to the wall against which it stands. Or it may mean a group of furniture, near or against a wall, or the shape of a rug against the floor. The ideal proportion has areas and shapes sufficiently alike to have something in common and still different enough to be interesting. The law of the ancient Greeks on proportion is still absolutely sound and the essence of simplicity. Two areas or lines have the most successful effect if one is more than one half and less than two thirds of the other.

You and your tastes must decide on the scale of your own living; but once it is established it must be consistent. If you are a dainty person you do not want oversized furniture any more than you want delicate pieces if you are large. A young bride came to me for help one time who had gotten herself into a silly jam with scale as a result of thoughtless and emotional buying. The marriage had not been a sudden one, and Mr. and Mrs. S. had casually discussed the kind of home they wanted—and that was all, since they had rented a summer cottage for the first month and expected to plan and assemble it then. Mr. S. was called away suddenly the day after they returned from their honeymoon and little Mrs. S. was forced to make all decisions regarding a place to live, and furnish it. She was under five feet and wore a size 10 dress. He was six feet three, a broad-shouldered, husky athlete. The apartment she found had a decent living room—14′ x 18′—but not a large one. In a post-honeymoon glow and with a heart full of love for this big husband of hers, she did her shopping. She bought nothing but large pieces of furniture and the result was disastrous. The room was bursting —not because there were too many pieces (she had planned that intelligently and carefully) but because they were all so overscaled. And poor little Mrs. S., completely out of scale with all of it, was engulfed when she sat in one of the chairs. Realizing that she couldn't cope, she came immediately for help, so that we were able to return the worst misfits without loss. Then we thought the problem through and selected most of the furniture on a medium scale so that one large comfortable chair for Mr. S. and a small one for Mrs. S. did not interfere with the over-all harmony of the room. This is an extreme case, but they were able to work it out and any family can fit their average size into the right scale. The size of most of our maturing young people is larger than in former generations and seems to be increasing. This indicates a need for sturdy backgrounds, but there are still many small people and probably will be for some time, so it is better not to get carried away by this trend, which is by no means universal.

COLOR CHART

showing value gradations of red and green

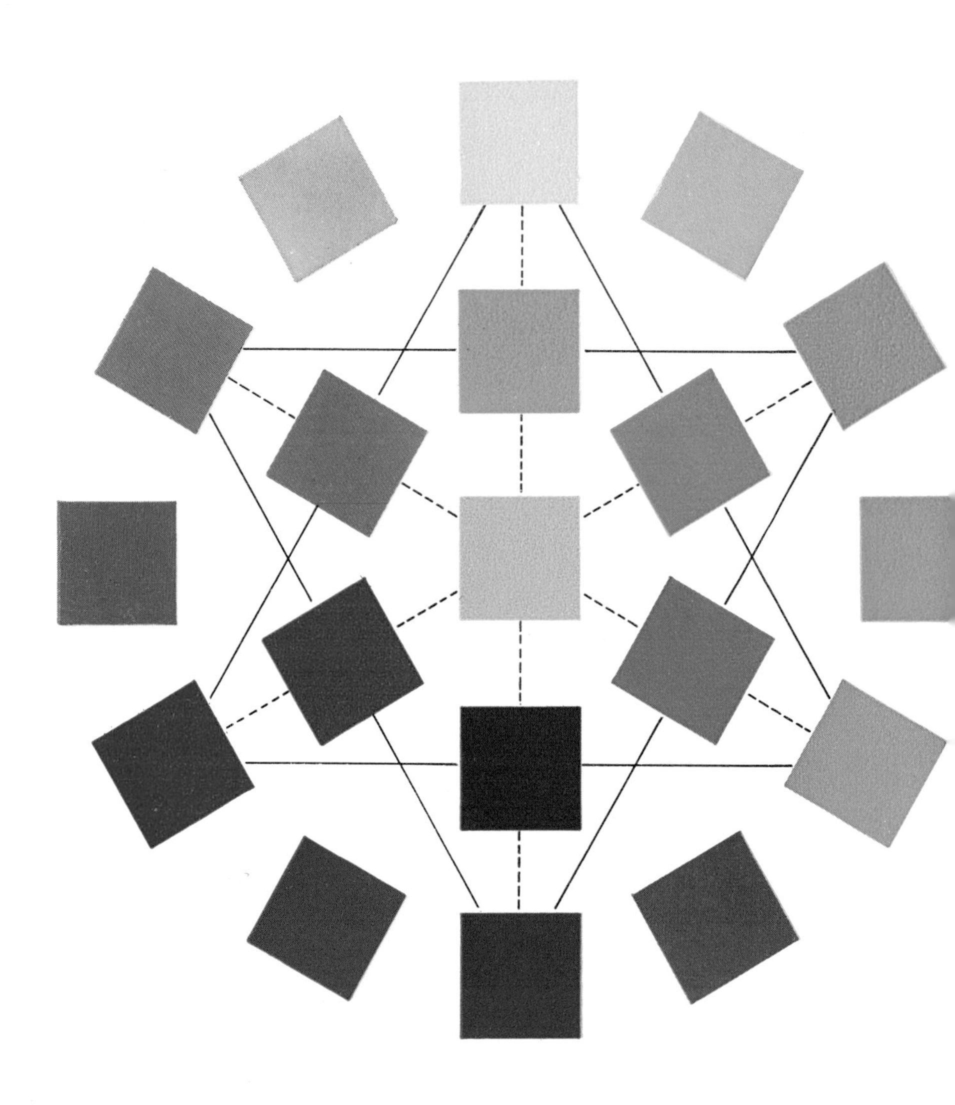

Traditional

Living room in *New York City*. French paneling of eighteenth-century design used with old chimney piece and furniture. DECORATOR, *Mary E. Dunn, A.I.D., for Nancy McClelland, Inc.*

EMILY HENRY BUSH

Traditional

Bedroom of house in *Hingham, Massachusetts.* Eighteenth-century house making use of traditional furniture in a comfortable and attractive room. DECORATOR, *Dorothy M. Powers, A.I.D.*

Combination of traditional and modern

Living room in *New York* apartment of a business woman. Modern room with both modern and antique furnishings. DECORATOR, *William Pahlmann, A.I.D., for William Pahlmann Associates.*

RUDI RADA

Combination of traditional and modern

Living room in *Miami Beach* house. Modern background making use of eighteenth-century French, Italian, and modern furnishings. DECORATORS, *James M. Smith, A.I.D., and James M. Wills, A.I.D., for James Merrick Smith Associates.*

Combination of traditional and modern

Living room in *New York* apartment. Modern background with modern furniture set off by a few old pieces and fine antique accessories. DECORATOR, *Edward J. Wormly, A.I.D.*

HUBE HENRY, HEDRICH-BLESSING

Modern

Living room in *Chicago* suburban house. A modern room with basic modern furnishings, comfortable and inviting. DECORATOR, *John C. Murphy, A.I.D., for Watson and Boaler, Inc.*

MAYNARD L. PARKER

Modern

Game Area of living room in modern house near *Los Angeles*. Modern furniture used in an indoor-outdoor room. Attractive and practical. DECORATOR, *Harold W. Grieve, A.I.D.*

Modern

Living room in house at *Lake Buchanan, Texas.* One end of a spacious, open modern room utilizing modern furniture. Free-form rug and table. DECORATOR, *Margaret Sedwick, A.I.D., for Margaret Sedwick Associates*

There are other things to watch out for on this matter of scale and proportion. A large side table should not be used with a small upholstered chair, nor a small chair, with delicate lines, at a large or heavy desk. Wherever you group furniture, be sure that the pieces have a basic common size. Scale is of tremendous importance in your pictures. Be sure the frames are right for the size and shape and don't overpower a small, softly colored painting with a heavy frame, nor try to frame a large one with a narrow molding. Always hang them with a scale relationship to their background. When you hang them over a piece of furniture, as is frequently the case, be certain that they are a harmonious size and shape and hang them close enough so the entire group will make a unit. When a painting is hung too high it is not only difficult to see but it has no connection with the piece under it and appears to be floating in space.

The scale of the pattern on a fabric should be right for the piece of furniture or window where it is to be used. Large wallpaper designs should not be crowded into small wall surfaces. If you have pattern on your floor, it must harmonize with the general feeling of sizes of the other things in the room. Be especially careful about your lamps. Functionally, large lamps are usually better than small ones, and although there are other things to consider, there is never any valid excuse for having them out of scale with your room. The scale of the shade should be the same as the lamp—an overpowering one on a small lamp is no worse than a tiny one on a large lamp. Both are horrible. Don't let your accessories get out of scale. They should not be too picky, but neither must they become too important as a result of size. Let design, color, and intrinsic interest give them their value—not scale.

The diversity of accessories as well as the places where they can be used is practically unlimited and your own personal inclinations in their use is equally infinite. This makes any kind of specific rules impossible, and general ones difficult. They are, and should be, a very direct expression of your personality, but use restraint. Subtlety, in their use, is always desirable. Avoid scattering and monotony and remember that they are intended to add to the decorative effect and not to confuse it. Plan their placement carefully, and except where you have a sound decorative reason for using something, don't let sentiment get the best of you. It is usually far better to have a need and fill it deliberately than to pick up things casually. When you have a large space to decorate, such as the top of a low bookcase or a mantel shelf, instead of dribbling things all the way across, plan a composition and group your objects so that they will help, rather than compete with, each other. Many people with sound taste on most matters are inclined to become confused on this one. For example, for your mantel you happen to have two rather slender candlesticks with no bulk, two medium-sized pieces of porcelain, and some kind of a fair-sized low bowl. Use the porcelain with the candlesticks—one each at either end—leaving the bowl in the center of enough space to give it importance. If you place all of them at regular intervals, none of them will contribute much to the appearance. This kind of generalizing can be dangerous, but when you are experimenting with any kind of an arrangement, such as dishes in a wall cupboard, remember that the spaces make the design almost as much as the objects (refer to the law of the Greeks in this chapter) and keep redoing it until it seems to hold together as one unit instead of going in all directions.

Form and line are so much a part of our understanding that it is difficult to define them. Form is made up of lines assembled to represent a shape—an area surrounded by lines. It is the basis for our recognition of an object—we identify a chair by its form. The contour of the object tells us what it is, if it is within our experience. This is not as quickly perceived as color because it requires an intellectual response in contrast to an emotional one. Good form depends on the same factors that are involved in good decorating—proper scale of forms to each other, proper proportion, unity, and balance. All forms used in your home should appear beautiful to you. Take a look and see if they do.

Form is made by lines but lines do not always result in complete forms. Line governs the shape of all flat areas and is the basis for all decorative ornament. Certain kinds of lines have definite qualities and can be used for specific effects. Horizontal lines are tranquil and fundamentally restful. Vertical lines are stronger and more structural; they seem to be ready for action. Diagonals seem to be pointing at something and must be used with care or they will keep the eye jumping. A circle or oval has movement, but the movement completes itself so is not restless. Used against a rectangle, such as the floor or wall of a room, they must be placed with care to avoid too much pattern. The safest use is as a repeat in a small area. A square completes itself and gives a feeling of solidity, and straight lines are also good where solidity is needed as they give a sturdy, strong feeling. A curved line is gayer, suggesting in its lighter forms an airiness and in its heavier ones a kind of transitory quality. Too many curves may produce a restless effect, but they are useful to relieve too many straight lines, which are inclined to make a room look stiff.

In the choosing and assembling of the elements of your home—furniture, wall coverings, assorted fabrics, floor treatments, and accessories, try to consider these basic qualities. With their guidance, build on the sound foundation of common-sense thinking and planning. Your entrance should welcome you and your guests—that is its main function. Think about this as you help some friend to thread her way through a back hall full of unattractive gear. A living room should be comfortable, convenient, restful, and attractive. Dining areas should be equipped with comfortable furniture, functional for its purpose, and the background should be a peaceful one. Bedrooms should also be peaceful and as roomy as possible, with ample storage space, proper lighting, and good mirrors. Kitchens may have gotten out of hand as far as common sense goes, but if there is any question concerning function, it would not be with lack of it.

Lighting is covered in this book only as it bears on the use of color in the home. This emphatically does not mean that it isn't an important aspect of the function and appearance of the home. On the contrary: but it is too big and too technical a subject to cover adequately here. One word of advice—it should be included as an essential part of your plans, and as early as possible: if you are building or remodeling, in the first projection of your ideas; if you are moving into an existing place, in your first tentative arrangements. It is certainly not incidental and you should consider all aspects—location, purpose, type of fixture best suited to function and appearance. Research is constantly being done by the lighting companies and the results are distributed through your light and power company. Problems vary locally and for specific information consult your local company. For a larger and more general need, go to your library and see what books they have on the subject. One of the best and most comprehensive books recently published is *How to Decorate and Light Your Home* by E. W. Commery, an engineering consultant for General Electric, in charge of residential lighting, and C. Eugene Stephenson, past president and chairman of the board of the American Institute of Decorators.

The information given in this chapter is simple and fundamental. There are no formulas for any of the real problems of the decorator. The sooner you abandon the idea that somewhere you will find the correct recipe for your own concoctions and decide to stick to sound principles, the sooner you will be on the right track. These principles won't let you down and through them you can create your home on the basis of good design. There seems to be a misconception about this among many people who are inclined to arrive at a solution by emotion—they "feel" what is good for them. This is 100-per-cent false. Knowing, and not feeling, will give you the right answer.

3

Color Is Incorruptibly Honest Learn Its Rules and Plan Your Own Schemes

Unquestionably, color plays the most important role in the decorative scheme—and the best part of it is that it is not only available, but cheap. Outside of speech, it is probably our most potent means of self-expression; the most used and the most abused. It is fascinating, tricky, and infinite in its possibilities. It depends mainly on an emotional response and since it is all around us, commonly within our experience, we make little effort to understand it. To get the most pleasure as well as the best use from color, it must be understood as well as felt. Even with a little understanding—and that is so very easy—you can make use of it in all kinds of exciting and constructive ways. It can cheer you up when you are sad, quiet your nerves when they are jumpy, or even pull you into a mood of depression. It can soften the effect of bad architecture or furniture and in fact is the only single element that can overcome bad features in form to make a room attractive. It can bring a room to life. And it has unlimited possibilities as a satisfying means of expressing your personality.

The number of combinations of colors is virtually limitless, the normal eye detecting around two thousand different colors. With this vast palette, a little understanding will certainly give you a better chance of success in your own expression. And with hundreds of shades of each color, it is dangerous to generalize. You may like blue with brown, but unless you have the right shades, blue and brown won't make a good color scheme. If you expect your final results to be the same as your original scheme, once a choice is made, keep a record of it. Color is treacherous and it is impossible to carry exact shades in your head (experts know better than to try). Avoid getting carried away by advertising and fashion promotion. Fads in color are fun, but their aim is to increase sales by convincing the public that they have something new and desirable. Color has been around for a long time. Let your own opinions guide you in your choice. It is better to have it right for you than to have it "smart."

The theory of color is confusing if you aren't a scientist or an expert. It isn't necessary for you to bother with that and what you need to know is best learned by experience. Ignoring theory, color is a natural science, governed by basic laws and rules, which make it much easier to understand. We know that it originates in light, and the fact that we have learned much about the controlling of light—both natural and artificial—in our homes, simplifies the project. The physicist considers color purely as light which can be mechanically subdivided through a prism and results in the familiar colors of the rainbow. For our purpose, color is made of pigment, or dyes, all of which we can use and can control completely. The theory that is generally accepted about the spectrum colors is that red, yellow, and blue are called primary colors because they cannot be reduced or subdivided. The secondary colors, orange, green, and purple, are an equal mixture of any two of the primaries, in three combinations.

The three general qualities which we must understand are hue, value, and intensity. Hue is simply the name of the color, which everyone understands. That is, they do unless our old friends the promoters are at work. One of the top gimmicks of any product that uses color is to manufacture seductive color names as a selling aid. Don't bite. This advice does not refer to any color name that is appropriately descriptive and good color names have frequently come out of this kind of promotion. But unless the name tells you something about the color, don't be taken in by it and especially if it sounds super-glamorous. One of the first "made" color names was Shocking Pink. Whether you liked it or not, you certainly knew what it was and it was so successfully pushed that the resultant overuse of it was unfortunate.

The quality of value denotes the amount of light or dark in a color or its place in a scale of even steps between white and black. If you have a primary red and want to make it stronger in value, it must be darkened. To make it weaker, lighten it. The correct use of value in creating a room contributes as much as any one component. The values must be so related that none is too important or aggressive and each increases the effectiveness of the others. If you can do this, your room will be harmonious in spite of other minor errors. In the simplest way, this means that your colors will all blend agreeably, with no extreme lights or darks jumping out at you.

Intensity means the amount of itself, or in our case, pigment, that the color contains. It is the degree of brightness and differs from value which is the degree of lightness or darkness. To make a color more intense, you have only to add more of the pure color and to make it less intense, you add white with an opaque paint such as we use on the wall, or plain water, with water colors. White added to a wall paint will not only decrease the intensity, it will slightly change the shade.

Many of our emotional reactions to color have crept into our speech—proof of their general acceptance. "Greenhorn" or "green as a gourd" describes the rank amateur. We can be "feeling blue" or "purple with rage." We can withdraw and be in a "brown study" or hear some startling news and "change color." We don't like to be "in the red" but we are always happy to be "in the pink."

The psychologists have long been interested in the effect of color on our thoughts and feelings. And just as there are basic laws and rules that govern the science, so there are for this, which means that in spite of its trickiness and seemingly runaway possibilities, it does have a code and sticks to it. It is a benign fact of nature that usually we react better to the colors we like and so are inclined to choose them to live with—a sound and practical idea.

Certain kinds of colors create definite feelings and effects. Red and orange are the two warmest colors and yellow the sunniest. Blues and greens are the most restful. Good mixtures of reds and yellows, in varying values, are always cheerful; of blues and yellows cool and peaceful; and of reds and blues either gay or dignified. The bright or lighter combinations of these which go toward the pinks are gay, either in a giddy or a subtle way. If they are closer to the purples, or the values darker, they can be dignified or cold and depressing. Cool colors make a wall recede and give a feeling of spaciousness, while warm colors are more aggressive and seem to come closer to you. Strong color fatigues the eye more than soft color and so must be used with caution. Be very careful of complementary colors (described in chart at end of chapter) used together, as the contrast between them is exaggerated and can give a room a restless quality.

Your use of color can determine the mood of your room. You can make it restful or restless, cheerful or dreary and gloomy, warm and inviting or cold and depressing. I once heard Dr. Howard Rusk, who is in charge of Rehabilitation at Bellevue Hospital in New York, describe the experiments they were making in the wards at Bellevue. The constructive and therapeutic benefits deriving from a little use of color were phenomenal.

Since color is completely dependent on light, your lighting must be considered from the beginning. Any good color that is fresh and not muddy will change greatly with different light, but it will remain a good color. In planning your colors you must consider the main function of the room and the kind of use. Will it be used more by day or by night? If by day, what kind of natural light does it have? If it is to be used in both lights, as many rooms are, select colors that change little in different light. If you are looking at them in a shop where the lighting is artificial, check to see what kind of lighting it is—fluorescent, daylight, regular or tinted bulbs. If it can be done, always arrange to take the sample home and try it in your own light. It is the only safe way because color is admittedly tricky and can look one way at the shop and entirely different in your home. The change that may take place in your reaction to a color after looking at it for a day must also be considered. It is a common occurrence for a color that has seemed devastating at the shop to turn into something undesirable after a day's viewing in your home. So take all precautions possible in making your selection.

Your number-one source of controlling natural light is your curtains—whether they are blinds, casement, or heavy-lined ones. This may come as a shock to persons who think of curtains as a basically decorative element. If you want light without bright sun, there are blinds that will filter it. There are many varieties to be found in this country, but the most functional ones are made in the old countries where they have had centuries of experience in keeping out the hot sun. The simplicity and efficiency of the blinds in the southern part of Europe so far exceeds anything we have here that it is a source of astonishment to me that their designs haven't been introduced in this country long ago. If you need to close off light from the top, you must have a blind that pulls down. If you want to close it vertically, any lined curtain, split bamboo, or wooden blind can cover whatever area you wish. But if you need air, be careful of a heavy curtain. Casement curtains can filter light, and can also, if you use color, change the tone of the light that comes through.

Artificial light is much easier to control, since you can determine the sources of your light to suit yourself in planning a room. If they already exist, you can still control the placing of your lamps. The most commonly used light bulbs cast a soft, yellow light. In addition to that bulb we have the daylight, which casts a cold, bluish-white light and the various tinted bulbs which will cast a soft glow of their own color. It is wise to experiment with whatever kind of lighting you intend to use before making any decisions about color.

The luminosity of a color should be considered and can be taken advantage of when light is inadequate. Many colors have a light-giving potential which is valuable when you need light but should be used with caution in houses with large picture windows that face on the sunny side. With so many large windows being used, it is wise to know the degree of luminosity your curtains will have. Yellow, which is most like the sun, has the most, followed by orange, which contains yellow. Green is next, and the more blue that is in the green the less luminous it is. Red is a hot color but not very luminous and blue and purple are useful in rooms that have too much light.

Lighting can also influence moods. Dark lights are more dignified than bright ones, which are gay and exhilarating. Soft lights are associated with romance and dim lights with mystery. Bright lights used with bright colors can be vulgar if badly done or exciting if expertly done. In the movie *Moulin Rouge,* Eliot Elisofon made the first use of this in a professional way by, as he said, "painting with light." He used warm coral filters to evoke the nostalgia of childhood scenes, fog filters to soften, and gray flashbacks and blue-green for the grim atmosphere of the attempted suicide. He used quantities of yellow and pink lights to create the sensually gay atmosphere of the cancan. All of these follow the rules of color, which are absolutely reliable.

Just as you wear colors that do the most for your complexion, hair, and general type, your background should complement you. Many redheads who love pink (most of them do) but can rarely wear it can get by with soft shades of it in their decorating schemes. Others prefer shades of green or brown. Whatever your kind of coloring, choose colors that do something for you when you start your planning. If there are color conflicts within the family, which often happens, work out a compromise for the rooms used by the family and go all out on your own room.

Where and how do you start to plan your color scheme? First and foremost, be sure that you are rested and relaxed. This is no notion. Color is stimulating and personal, and it requires genuine interested concentration. You can NOT make right decisions when you are fatigued. Don't work too long with it or try to make a lot of decisions at one time. When you start you may find that everything seems to be simple and goes very well: later it becomes an effort. That is the time to stop. Go at it again when you are enthusiastic and fresh. As in any decorating plan, aim high. Even if you do have to make some compromises, the final result will be more satisfying.

There are specific things that color can and should do for a room. The first is to build a satisfactory aesthetic effect. It should also express the personality of the person or persons who are to live there and contribute to the "certain feeling" or desired character that you have in mind. Start with your floor plan after you have made a tentative selection of furniture and have it placed. From this consider your areas. As important as the scheme itself is the relationship of areas—proportion again. Your largest area is your background—floor and walls—which should do just what the name suggests, stay back. Usually it is best to use quiet or neutralized colors in these areas; it takes an expert to use the stronger ones. The smaller the area, the brighter the color may be, generally speaking, and if that is what you like. Rooms can be beautiful without any bright colors and that is a matter of personal preference. If you do like them, confine them to accessories, on the whole, but be just as careful in selecting these colors as those for the larger areas. A small brilliant accessory can attract more attention in a room than a large sofa done in a soft, neutral color. The object is to plan your areas so that no one will stand out. Instead, there will be a feeling of unity which will ensure a harmonious room. Keep it simple and don't try to use too many colors.

Be sure that the colors you choose are suitable for the way you plan to use them. Avoid red for a library, and dark, somber tones for any kind of a family room. Scale and proportion are important in this matter of suitability. A delicate pink tone is out of place on a large lounge chair—save it for the small boudoir chair in your bedroom. The use of dark or heavy colors on small pieces is also bad. You can completely destroy the right effect by covering a piece with an unsuitable color.

The classic example of suitable use of color is found in the historic periods of design. Each one is characterized by certain colors which were ideally suited to the kind of rooms and furniture, and the way of life of the times. In the grand and overdecorated palaces of Louis XIV, you will see dark colors—reds, greens, and blues and a great deal of gold, exactly right for the heavy scale of both rooms and furnishings. During the reign of Louis XV the scale was lighter, furniture became more comfortable, and the colors were much softer. There was much use of wood paneling, finished either in its natural tone of soft brown or painted a delicate off-white or gray, with the moldings in gold—a much less ornate gold than the earlier period. The grays were actually very light and muted cool colors —blues or greens or mauves. Under the influence of Marie Antoinette, the Louis XVI period expressed a more classic and orderly kind of design. The rooms were smaller, the life less elegant, and the colors very quiet. Again much use was made of off-whites and although colors were still used, none was strong or bright. After the Revolution, patriotism was popular and the red, white, and blue of the French flag was used in many gay combinations. Empire green has been used so much in this country in recent years that most of us are familiar with it. Other colors of the Empire period, all of which were perfectly suited to the designs, were grayed purples, dull blues and mustardy browns. All of these colors were subtle ones and not haphazardly arrived at. The eighteenth-century English colors were equally suitable—softly neutralized blues, greens, and browns. The Adam brothers, who had a strong influence on their times, were partial to light gray with a blue or mauve cast, used with white and a pale chartreusy green. In the furniture the woods that set off these colors ranged from a light satinwood to a dark mahogany. Gold was used with restraint. Our own Colonial colors were varied but few of them were bright. Fairly strong colors were used in fabrics and wallpapers but they were usually slightly neutralized, and not at all dull.

If your house or apartment is large, you can use a greater variety of colors than is possible in a smaller one. Consider the purpose of the room. Will it be used for living, eating, playing, sleeping, or working? What kind of a background are you building? Do you want it peaceful or stimulating, warm or cool, luxurious or severe, casual or formal? What is the exposure? The geographical location is important as well as the type of community. An Iowa farmhouse could have something in common with one in New England or even in Texas, but it would not fit into an industrial community. The climate is always with us and must be considered.

This house or apartment is for you and your family and your personal tastes must govern your choice. It is usually easier to develop your scheme starting with some specific object—possibly a favorite painting or a wallpaper or fabric. It would be a good idea if each member of the family would bring to the planning conference some object or color for which he has a special attachment.

You have decided the kind of room you want, assembled possible color samples, and you are ready to make a tentative choice. Some colors are easier to work with than others and it is well to remember that the brighter the color and the sharper the contrast, the more difficult it is to work out a successful scheme. The first matter to consider is the choice of a background, which will be the largest area. Consider the size, and remember exposure and lighting. In choosing your colors it is imperative that you realize that they appear much lighter and less intense in a small sample, such as you will be using, than they do on the wall. You can learn this through bitter experience, but if you are wise you will see a sample of your wall color that is at least six feet high and two or three feet wide. The opposite is true of very light colors—soft tones that have little color in them. They will appear lighter in a large area. If any texture is involved, such as a rough wall, nubby fabric, etc., the color will appear darker; and a shiny surface which reflects will make it seem lighter.

In nature we are accustomed to a general gradation of values—from light above us to darker below—light sky, middle tones in the distance, and stronger and deeper ones below us. A light ceiling, intermediate walls, and a darker floor is the natural arrangement and the easiest for an amateur to use successfully. Unless you have colors that are actually bad, it will look well. However, it is not the only way and any good decorator can juggle these values and create a variety of combinations. In the room shown in color preceding page 121 there is a slight variation. The main color interest is in the oriental rug and the other colors are chosen to complement it. The walls are lighter in value and the high ceiling is painted a slightly darker tone, which makes it more interesting and brings it down. This is an example of a good place to paint architecture a different value and to make it more important. The cornice, different from the other architecture in the room, is a fine enough one to be featured. The table cover is not intended to be too prominent and is close to the value of the chair. The wood tone contrasts with the background, which makes it show up that much better. The rug provides enough color so that little is needed in the accessories—a small bouquet of flowers and one of the paintings. It all holds together harmoniously—furniture and colors.

Too many colors in a room can be not only displeasing but actually disturbing. Keep your schemes simple and see how much you can do with a few colors. One of the most successful rooms I ever did had one wall color and one fabric. The wall was painted in a soft, warm, and light pinky-beige, with a deeper tone used on a very high ceiling to bring it down. The fabric, used for curtains and all upholstery, was a red print on a natural linen. The furniture in the room was a variety of hand-me-downs, some nice and some ordinary. By keeping the scheme simple, I was able to give the room harmony and the dignity that it needed.

The size and shape of a room should help to determine the kind of color. A long narrow room can be made to look wider if the end walls are brighter than the side walls. A small room will look larger if a soft, cool color is used, making the walls recede. The height of a low room may be exaggerated by the use of strong verticals—panels, interesting tall bookcases, wallpaper, or any good decorative design with a strong vertical direction. If the ceiling is too high, a wallpaper molding called a dado can be applied about three feet or three and a half feet from the floor to break the height with its horizontal line. A dark color will bring a high ceiling closer and a light color pushes a low one up. Where bad architectural features exist, such as unsightly beams or breaks in the wall near the ceiling, it is usually best to paint the ceiling the same as the walls. This will help to conceal the defects. Any room that is cluttered up with a lot of architecture that isn't good should be painted one quiet color—including all woodwork. Lines that are not good should always be painted the same as the walls. On the other hand, if you have beautiful architectural features that you want emphasized, they can be painted a darker or lighter tone of your wall color—or, in rare cases, a contrasting color. But be sure they deserve it; it is very difficult to do it well.

Just as there are no pat formulas for the design problems of decorating, there are none for the color problems. You can be inspired and helped with ideas and suggestions for your color schemes, but you must make the final choice—on the basis of your own preference, plus your knowledge and whatever experience you have. But there are certain practical factors already mentioned that I want to summarize. Don't fool with color decisions when you are tired. Let your first consideration be the purpose of the room, including every phase of its use. Experiment as much as possible, bringing samples home to try. Whatever your inspiration or starting point, work from it and choose your background colors first, floor, walls, and ceiling; your secondary colors such as curtains or larger pieces of furniture next, and your accents last. It is much easier to match a paint color to a fabric or wallpaper than vice versa, so after your tentative background choice, have your wallpapers or fabrics on hand when you make your final selection. Never try to carry a color in your head. Try your colors in all types of lighting to be used and be sure that your trial areas are sufficiently large. Be sure that your colors are suitable and that the scale of pattern is correct for its use. Never use a color without a good reason and, above all, keep your schemes simple.

COLOR CHART

Color is what it is and there is no fooling around with it. What one color does to another is governed by its laws just as surely as the earth is subject to the force of gravity. There is much that you can do with it if you are interested enough to learn its laws. The way to learn how to control it is by experimenting, and only through experience can you develop a sound understanding of the effect of colors on each other—mixed together or used together. Truly, it will open your eyes to all kinds of wonderful things. The quickest way to develop this understanding is to start with the primary colors and build your own chart. You can learn this best through doing it.

Go to your nearest art supply store and get either a small box of water-color paints or small tubes of student paints. Look at their color chart and pick what you consider the truest red, yellow, and blue. The names may mean nothing to you, so choose by color. At the end of the book there is a list of these names with a description to help you identify them as to family or hue. You will need some fairly heavy water-color paper—a child's sketch pad will do. Get an inexpensive brush and some blotters and you are ready to start.

In Chapter 2 there is a completed chart; refer to it as you go. All color starts with the three primary colors on this chart, and in our project everything is the result of cause and effect. For your first three colors, mix enough water with the paint so you can try it on the paper. Get it as strong as possible—these should be true colors—and use the chart as an approximate guide. Make several samples of each, large enough to make a one-inch square. On a large piece of paper make a six-sided star, allowing six inches to each triangle side. Cut your squares from your best samples and place the yellow one at the top, the red one at the left corner of that triangle, and the blue at the right. From here on, all colors are combinations of these original ones. Our next one, gray, will include all three primaries, in equal amounts. Your paints may not be accurate, but use your own judgment. Place this square in the center.

Mix your orange next—theoretically equal parts of red and yellow. Place this square on the point at the upper left of the star. Green, made from equal parts of yellow and blue, goes on the upper right, and purple, the same mixture of red and blue, goes at the bottom. These colors make up the spectrum and our half tones fill the spaces between them: yellow-orange, with more yellow than red, red-orange, red-purple, blue-purple, blue-green and yellow-green. These color names are descriptive. When this circle is filled you have the twelve basic hues.

All of these colors are arrived at by mixing colors next to each other. Now we come to the combinations that are opposite each other on the chart. These are called complements and the normal complement of a color is the one containing the primary colors not in the original one. On the chart, complements are opposite each other: green is the complement of red as it contains yellow and blue which are no part of red. Orange is the complement of blue, purple of yellow, etc. In mixing, a color grays or neutralizes its complement—a most important fact to remember. The more of its complement it contains, the grayer or more neutral it becomes; equal parts of the three primaries make a true gray. Make only six neutralized colors, as in the chart.

So, we see that colors near each other on the chart produce another color, but without any neutralizing. Colors opposite each other have an entirely different effect and always neutralize each other. There are as many complements as there are hues. Complements used next to each other in a scheme give the maximum of contrast and must be carefully thought out.

Color harmonies or schemes are based on likeness or contrast; also called related or complementary. There are two kinds of related schemes: 1. those based on variations of one hue, going from a deep gray-green in the carpet to a soft and lighter one on the wall, or 2. analogous variations of one primary base—all hues from green through green-blue, but not including blue. There are several kinds of contrasting schemes but the two most commonly used (the rest get very complicated) are: 1. complementary, which is based on any pair of complements in varying shades. This must be handled carefully, using grayed shades for large areas and only where strong contrast is needed, using the colors at their full intensity; 2. double complementary, which includes two hues that are side by side on the chart, such as yellow and yellow-green and their respective complements—the purples and blue purples, but not the red. As you can see, the more complicated the type of scheme, the more dangerous it is to fool with it. Simple schemes can be as beautiful as more involved ones, so be careful to take on only what you can handle.

This is all very simple to do, and so very rewarding to have done. What you learn becomes a part of your experience and you can always refer to it, right there, in working with colors. Good luck and have fun.

4
If You Use a Decorator

This profession of ours—that of interior designer and decorator—has been consistently and repeatedly misunderstood. Why—and is it justified? I believe it is mainly due to a combination of misinformation and lack of information. Certainly a tremendous amount of misinformation has been circulated. Also, as in any profession, the minority of unethical members can give a bad name to the majority of honest and sincere ones.

Let's first be certain exactly what a decorator is and then examine the current crop of misinformation. Miss Nancy McClelland, a pioneer in the field and one of the finest of decorators, first defined it as, "One who by training and experience is qualified to plan, design, and execute structural interiors and their furnishings, and to supervise the various arts and crafts essential to their completion." The American Institute of Decorators, a national organization of qualified interior designers, founded in 1931 for the purpose of developing and maintaining high standards of quality and ethical practices, has taken over this definition as its official one. Mr. Richard Bach, Educational Consultant for the A.I.D., has for a number of years been working with representatives of the Department of Labor in an effort to replace an inadequate definition with an accurate, specific, and complete one. The result of this is the following definition released during the past year by the Bureau of Labor Statistics Dictionary of Occupational Titles: "Interior Designer and Decorator (including consulting decorator) designs, plans, and furnishes interiors of houses, commercial and institutional structures, hotels, clubs, ships, theatres, as well as set decoration for motion-picture arts and television. Makes drawings and plans of rooms showing placement of furniture, floor coverings, wall decorations, and determines color schemes. Furnishes complete cost estimate for client's approval. Makes necessary purchases, places contracts, supervises construction, installation, finishing and placement of furniture, fixtures, and other correlated furnishing and follows through to completion of project."

During the past year the New York Chapter of the A.I.D. planned a meeting to hear what other people thought of them—mainly publicity people. Mr. Alfred Auerbach, a public relations specialist and a close analyst of design trends, started his talk to us with what he called the five myths concerning decorators.

MYTH I A decorator is overbearing, disdainful, snobbish, and superior. He (or she) has all the taste and culture—the client has none. Retain a decorator and you are strait-jacketed into accepting an artificial stiff interior in which you may not move a pincushion without disturbing the music of the planets. (Unquote—they never should have mentioned that pincushion as it proves we are functional.)

MYTH II A decorator not only disregards the taste of the client, he (or she) pays little heed to the practical realities of life. Unrealistic solutions are developed which stifle natural family life—i.e., for a while—for soon there is rebellion as human needs and habits come into play. The room or the home subsequently is altered bit by bit and after a while the inhibiting touch of a decorator is kicked out of the room.

MYTH III Decorators are interested only in designing châteaux, mansions and penthouses (unquote—didn't know there were enough to go around). They would not dream of decorating just a living room in a suburban home or working on a two-room underfed apartment in Manhattan or Long Island. (Unquote—try us and see.)

MYTH IV Mrs. Jones seems to feel that using a decorator costs a lot of money. Decorators bombard their clients into helpless acquiescences (unquote—and some *decorators* take a REAL beating) and propel purchases far beyond the original budget. Call in a decorator and you'll be swimming in debts for years and years.

MYTH V Decorators are poor organizers. They take forever and a day to complete a project—no one here, of course!

As is obvious, I hope, these are too extreme to be taken seriously and he proceeded to disprove them. As he pointed out, any slight basis in fact existed a long time ago, comparatively speaking, in the evolution of this rather recent profession.

Decorators are human beings, and just as lawyers and doctors vary in the caliber of their service—both as to ability and standards—so do decorators. But they ARE people who are interested in the business of creating right backgrounds for living and who have qualified themselves to do so by specialized training. They are willing to devote their time to making a living at it and, contrary to the notions of many people, it is NOT a glamorous profession but a very demanding one.

Too many people think of a decorator as someone who is paid a lot of money to make a house or an apartment look beautiful. This is far from the case. In the first place, it is the job of the decorator to save you money. Although it is certainly important to have the home as attractive as possible, this is by no means the only aim. The total goal is the satisfaction and comfort of the people who are to live there—and this includes the physical and visual comforts as well as the intellectual ones. In other words, it includes everything that contributes to the usefulness and enjoyment of the room. This involves selection of all the ingredients that go to make up the furnishings of a room—color, fabrics, furniture, wall coverings, and accessories. Every day of the year sees new products appearing on the market, glowingly described by their advertising. The decorator has a much better opportunity to evaluate these products than the consumer—in fact it is one of his primary responsibilities. It is his job to know which ones can make the most practical as well as the most satisfactory contribution to the projects at hand. Obviously an expert should be able to do this better and more economically than any amateur.

Most decorators do not charge for their time. They are in business as the middleman to sell to you, retail, the products which they buy from the wholesaler. This is exactly what the grocer does —or any merchant that you trade with—except that they don't have such a responsibility for guiding your selection. The myth that it costs more to use a decorator is a very frequently aired one, but it won't cost you more unless *you* decide that you want it that way. Haven't you ever, when you went to buy a coat, learned facts about wear or durability or some phase of use that prompted you to spend more than you had originally intended? You don't go home and say that the salesperson cost you more money, do you? It is true that often you learn to understand phases of structure or design and realize that by spending more at this point you will save money later; and this certainly is legitimate. If the decorator does try to sell you a big bill of goods simply to increase his profit, you have the wrong decorator and will soon know it. Find another. If the doctor started recommending operations to pad his own purse, you would do the same thing.

Some decorators work on a consultation or fee basis. They charge for their time and if they are worth consulting at all, their time is valuable. One client came to me for consultation to see if I could advise him as to how he could better "make do" with a living room with which he was just about 100-per-cent dissatisfied. He planned to do a complete job of decorating but had just bought the house and all his resources were going into a terrace, patio, carport, etc. I made two trips to his home and on the basis of this consultation he managed, not too unhappily, to wait until he was ready to go ahead. The room was an awkward shape, with a fireplace right beside one window and difficult wall spaces. For this temporary solution every bit of training and experience I had had plus all available brain power were needed—much more than the amount required for a regular decorating job. Remember, we weren't buying a thing.

In his basement I found a clean, metal barrel and a couple of square tea canisters—neither old nor decorated, but a good size. He brought the barrel into the living room and on a piece of heavy cardboard I drew an oval approximately 22" x 34", which he cut out. We put it on top of the barrel and covered it with a carefully draped sheet. With one comfortable chair and his best lamp, it filled the wall space opposite the fireplace nicely. I suggested that he dip the sheet in a gray dye or tint and cut it off at the floor, which he did. One more wall piece was needed and the desk from the adjoining room was moved in. It filled the other wall space in exactly the right way and wasn't missed in the smaller room, which didn't need it anyway. His sad little love seat was moved into a spot where it was not only more functional but actually did something for the room. The fireplace looked very dreary, with a dark picture hung horizontally, centered, and a pair of bottles balanced neatly at the ends. We turned the picture vertically, placed it off center, and found some interesting jugs in the kitchen cupboard that completed the arrangement and all he had to do was replace the painting with another one, using the same frame. The tea canisters were used for lamps and by adding wooden bases he gave them essential height and importance; with shades of the proper scale, they were simple, good design.

The rest of the furniture was arranged to make the most of the one large window with a view, as well as the decorative possibilities of the books in the built-in bookcases. The room had lost its hopeless quality and its feeling of complete disorganization and had become more functional. This kind of makeshift is not to be recommended as the right answer to anything. But during the two years while the land was being terraced down to the river, a beautiful patio built, and all kinds of expensive planting added, his living room was much more attractive and comfortable. The room has now been completed and we were able to make use of a lot of our early trial and error in arrangement, etc. It has been painted, has new curtains, a new love seat and chair, new lamps, two small tables, slip covers on the old chairs, a handsome old drop-leaf table, and four very attractive side chairs (which I found and he bought) and pictures that are right, which it particularly needs.

I know that he felt that what he had paid for that early consultation was more than worth while, and as for me, I never did send him a bill for the hours I spent pondering the problems of that cockeyed room. Any ethical decorator will give you much more than you pay for when you have nothing to buy and need only advice on color, arrangement, or some other specific problem.

Remember that the decorator must put his entire mind to the solution of your problems as economically and practically as possible. This requires knowledge and concentration. I have had clients pay a fee which I had earned, and then expect to be able to call and pick my brain on the phone at will—and for an unlimited length of time. This is definitely unfair and a very difficult thing to stop in a tactful way. A reliable person will give you more than your money's worth in the first interview and grabbing for more is strictly unethical.

How, then, do you discriminate in selecting your decorator? First, if you have had an architect whose work you have liked, his recommendation should be a sound one. If your architect and decorator work together, it undoubtedly increases your chances of satisfactory results. And in any case, the sooner you call in the decorator, the better in the long run. Select your decorator just as you would a specialist in any field. Learn all you can about him—by his reputation, which can easily be checked, and by the kind of work he does. Be sure to see either actual rooms that he has done or photographs of his work. Listen to as much talk as you like, but never allow yourself to be talked into using a decorator. Don't let any reasoning affect your reactions to the visual approach. Don't ever choose anyone about whom you have any reservations, and don't bother with anyone for whom you don't feel a sincere liking. The personalities in this relationship will have to understand each other and if there is any clash at all, it will certainly cause trouble and may disrupt the whole deal.

Before you approach a decorator, have all of your ideas coordinated and organized in your own mind. There are many decisions that do not involve him and can be made before you consult him—such as the amount of money you plan to spend, the specific function of each room, as well as the assignment of a room to an individual, where this is to be done. This kind of thing can be decided in your family discussions and you can tell, if you care, exactly what it is your job to decide before presenting your problems to the decorator. Pasteur has said that "chance favors the prepared mind." In this case your preparation is simply a practical means of leaving as little as possible to chance.

It will be helpful to make lists of things that you especially like and just as important to list the things you really don't like. With the best of intentions, no decorator can know this without being told. I will never forget one of my first jobs of shopping on which I had worked hard in assembling what I thought was an attractive and appropriate scheme for a sitting room for a lady. When I presented it, she said, "It is very nice—but I never use anything with a floral pattern." How simple it would have been if she had told me first! This is the place where your carefully saved clips, which should be together in your scrapbook, will be very useful. Your decorator will understand any of your photographs better than all of the word-built pictures in the world.

Practice making up your mind. You don't want your decorator to tell you what to do—and he doesn't really want to either. But when you can't make up your mind, this is apt to happen simply to get things going, and if you have been procrastinating, it is as much your responsibility as it is his. It won't be easy, so be prepared for that; in everyday living you don't have as many or as serious decisions to make in such a brief time. Be sure you have explored the possibilities adequately and have taken sufficient time to consider carefully—and then make up your mind. It is somewhat like mediation between labor and management—it has to be done sometime and the sooner (as long as you are careful) the better. The business of indecision can become a chronic disease at this time if you let it. One client of mine had an advanced case of this. Unfortunately, she had access to the trade magazines, where new products frequently appear long before they are available on the market. Everything that caught her eye had to be explored so that decisions were postponed interminably and time wasted to the point where it was impossible to show any profit on the job. So avoid that, but, on the other hand, don't go to the other extreme and decide just to get things moving. Chronic indecision as I have had occasion to observe it in a client is something quite apart from the difficulty of a choice between two ideas or articles. You will know which is your trouble, and even at the expense of a little delay (be reasonable) be certain that you really like everything that goes into your schemes. This is for you and you are the final judge of it and don't forget it for a second.

There are no legal limitations to the use of the title "interior decorator." Anyone who chooses to can hang up a shingle with that name on it and make like a decorator. It is the aim of the A.I.D. to achieve the same standard of official acceptance for the decorator as has been worked out for architects—licensing. In architecture this is under state control, but there are regulations in every state with fairly uniform standards of practice and ethics. Licensing in this field began in the larger cities, as very specific building standards became necessary for human safety. The American Institute of Architects is the organization accepted as setting the standards in the field and in most states is called in to supervise examinations. A degree is necessary and, following that, several years of practical experience before it is possible to pass the exam, which also covers in detail local building codes and regulations. There is not the safety element in decorating that there is in architecture, but the A.I.D. is plugging for licensing as a protection to the consumer, and if we can accomplish this, no one who can't pass a similar examination will be permitted to call himself an interior decorator or designer.

In the meantime, how can you guard yourself against being taken in by a self-termed decorator? In addition to using common sense and proceeding as I have suggested above, you can check the background and knowledge of the individual against the definition given by the Department of Labor. Your decorator should be able to do everything on that list. But do note that the list, simplified, is as follows: designs, makes drawings and plans of rooms, furnishes complete cost estimate, makes purchases, places contracts, etc. This involves a complete job and the decorator is responsible to you for the satisfactory completion of the work. That is his responsibility and don't expect him to estimate your yardage offhand—the job of the curtain or upholstery workroom—nor to explain details of construction. It is his job to plan and be responsible for the execution—not to immerse himself in the details. Too many people expect the decorator to know the specific items which are left to the workmen responsible for them. His mind should be on the planning and the execution of the job and should not be cluttered up with that kind of detail.

A word of caution. Avoid the people who offer to "get it for you wholesale." Avoid the so-called 10-per-centers who offer to do it for less. Just apply to them the same standards you apply to any business. They may not be dishonest (or they may be) but in any case, the procedure is not ethical.

And what about the decorator? Who is to protect him from his clients when they are unreasonable, too demanding or greedy? There isn't anyone and there are many times when it would be a good thing if there were. Just remember that you aren't the only person whose problems he is struggling with, and that he is not superhuman but just an individual who has the same troubles getting things done as the rest of the world. A little consideration and an appreciation of some of the obstacles can be soothing to the relationship and a real help in getting things accomplished. Clients can be cruelly thoughtless in their demands and completely unreasonable in their schedule of execution. You wouldn't be that kind of a client—would you?

5

When You Move Your Home

One of the most common household problems to be coped with these days is sudden and/or arbitrary moves. Twenty-five years ago, moving, as a business, scarcely existed. Today it is done on a huge scale as shown by the many large companies equipped to do the complete job of moving household possessions —either across the town or the country. The development of our technological civilization has made the static life of the past century completely obsolete.

Moving is a job that no one can really do for you. The physical packing and transportation can be taken care of by people especially trained to do it, which can relieve your mind at a time when it is truly overloaded. But previous to having that done, you have had to find a place to move into, mentally adjust your possessions in the new setup, and plan its accomplishment. This will involve many decisions, including the intensely painful one as to what is to be kept and what discarded. After the move you have the job of organizing and settling your things into their new environment. The most frequent of these moves can be listed under four general headings: 1. rental to ownership, 2. ownership to rental, 3. large to small, and 4. small to large. None of them is easy and the experience of someone who has been through it can be of help. I have chosen a common move from each of these headings to illustrate an average situation and its solution. From these descriptions you should be able to collect some helpful and practical ideas. Any of them can involve old or new and modern or traditional.

A move frequently made is from a city apartment which is rented to a house in the country which has been purchased. In an average three-room apartment, which includes a living room, with dining foyer, bedroom, small kitchen, and bath, there might be the following furniture: living room—1 Lawson sofa, 1 large upholstered chair, 1 upholstered chair with ottoman, 1 small upholstered chair, 1 Victorian rocker, 2 matching cabinets for radio and Hi-Fi, 1 coffee table, 2 end tables, 1 butterfly table, 1 nest of tables, 1 small chest of drawers, 3 lamps, 1 large rug, 2 side chairs and a TV. In the foyer perhaps a small rug, a day bed, a drop-leaf table, a hutch and 4 dining chairs. The bedroom may contain 1 fair-sized rug, 1 double bed, 2 bedside tables, 2 dressers—not matching ones—1 desk, 1 desk chair, and 1 upholstered chair. The house you are moving into is a modern one, built on a hill, with living room, dining room, kitchen and lavatory on the second floor and three bedrooms and a bath on the first.

There are a number of ingenious expedients which will make your furniture fill more space. The butterfly table, which, closed, is approximately 14" x 22", can be opened to its full oval and covered with a large piece of felt fitted to hang to the floor. Instead of a light, leggy piece, you have a substantial and solid wall piece. The nest of tables, about the same size, but squarer, can be used against the wall in the dining room, with a fairly large picture hung slightly low over it and on it a good-sized vase full of green leaves, which can usually be brought in from outside, except for a few months of the year. On the smallest dining-room wall, the two side chairs of good design can be placed together to give the appearance of a larger piece of furniture. The bedside tables, actually small chests, can be put together on one wall of the bedroom with an interesting painting of good scale to make a perfectly satisfactory group. New and smaller ones may be purchased to use beside the bed, unpainted, and later all the wood pieces painted one color. With these chests, only one dresser is needed in this bedroom and the other can go into the smallest bedroom. The day bed and the desk and chair and upholstered chair from the original bedroom may be used in the third bedroom, which has a fireplace and can become a combination study and TV room. A small bookcase from the town kitchen can go into the small bedroom, which becomes a guest room, with the addition of twin beds—your only expensive purchase. Your house will not only look furnished but it will be comfortable as well as attractive. If you can do it this way—make what you have furnish the house—you can take all the time you need in choosing the things you add and consequently be sure they are right.

In any move it is problematical as to the re-using of old curtains. In some cases the windows are totally different both as to size and shape. Here the bedroom curtains might be used in the guest room, and for the rest of the house—modern, with many windows and a magnificent view—new ones will be needed. If there is not a lot of difference in size, often curtains can be adjusted and used as well after the move as before, since they are still being used with the same furniture.

The move from a large house to a small apartment that I am using involves a furnished apartment. As is frequently the case—especially where the change may not be permanent—a difficult aspect is the elimination of everything that will not be needed until later. After many years in the one house, the children leave, and when the death of the husband leaves the wife alone she may try staying on. How long this lasts will vary, but after two years the wife in my case was convinced that it wouldn't work. She planned eventually—in fifteen or possibly twenty years—to settle in the town where one of her children lived. Her problem was one that is faced by many women these days and she coped with it in a very intelligent way.

The first and most onerous task was to decide just what she would discard. She started by going through each room—first sorting what was to be kept and what disposed of on a quick-decision basis. As the piles that were to be discarded grew, she had to re-sort it and then figure out the best way to dispose of it. She looked into the possibilities thoroughly and chose the public auction. As she did not have enough discards to make her own sale, she located a place where she could take them to be sold with the relics of other displaced people. This may seem a very painful way to get rid of your property, much of which has nostalgic and sentimental value, but actually she found it a very good way. The dates are set ahead, there is no time to feel sorry about the whole situation—nor for yourself—and when the day comes, everything is done in such a matter-of-fact way that it seems to be over with quickly. If you have fewer things, you can advertise them in the papers, or if you have valuable ones you can take them to a good auction gallery. You can even have your own auction if you think you have enough possessions to dispose of. This is for you to decide.

The things she chose to keep had to go into storage, since she expected to live in a different community during the next years. Under these circumstances it is essential to consider everything very carefully. In order to be worth keeping in storage, an object must be of more value to you, either in a practical or a sentimental way, than the cost of storage. It is sometimes cheaper to replace the old things with new ones than to store them, so this requires thoughtful weighing. Also, be very sure that you don't dispose of anything that you really do want to keep, something that is—either for practical or sentimental reasons—irreplaceable.

She ended up by giving a few of the nice old things to her family, storing a very few that she truly cherished and that certainly, to her, were irreplaceable, and putting aside things that she would use wherever she was—linen, a few dishes, and a minimum of kitchen equipment. The new kitchen merchandise was so superior to hers that it seemed foolish to keep any of it but she did hang on to her usable electrical equipment. Most important, and really essential to her happiness, were her books and she planned to take some with her. Even these she culled and then selected which were to go to storage, which were to be disposed of (this was especially painful), and which were to go with her. None of this was easy.

But when you eliminate in this sensible and thoughtful way, what you do keep will surely show, in your home, a distillation of you and of your personality.

And it certainly did in this case. The furnished apartment she moved into was a dilly and nothing but pure essence would have made any impression, although she was able to make a few small changes. The apartment had the essentials that were very hard to find at that time. The location and the plan of the rooms were both good. But the decoration! It really took courage for her to sign the lease, but she has not, to this day, regretted it. Along with the essentials she has a kind and accommodating landlord and more than a fair amount of comfort and convenience. In order to dull the impact of the design, she has made a few changes.

At the time she moved in the wallpaper was violently figured and both rugs and curtains had a very noticeable pattern. The living room had a "Jumbo modrenne" suite that was horrible in design, but still upholstered in a monotone and quite comfortable to sit on. The room was irregular and all of the furniture was huge in scale and consequently seemed crowded together. The first thing she got rid of was the figured rug, replacing it with a plain and inexpensive cotton one in a soft beige. This took care of the floor and the rug didn't have to be large as the floor was painted a dark color that was a good background. Next came the curtains—ready-made, in a simple fabric and a deeper shade of beige. Except for the sofa and large chair, all of the other furniture gradually went out and was replaced by extremely light and simple wicker—well designed. For her books she got black wire cases that are completely inconspicuous. Someone gave her a flat-top desk that is by no means beautiful, but it is simple and besides being useful, it adds a little character to the room. She likes and enjoys plants but has limited the number in the room so that those she has are decorative. She has replaced fancy lamps with decent but inconspicuous ones and has, with great patience and care, managed to hang pictures that are not overpowered by the wallpaper.

Her bedroom, fortunately, never did get all gussied up and she had only to replace the figured curtains with plain ones. The furniture is adequate and plain. The hall has an unpainted chest that harmonizes well with the paper (no pattern) and, other than a phone cabinet, which is filled with magazines, she has nothing except one wall of maps. Everything she has done is the result of thoughtful planning, never forgetting the importance of simplicity, keeping all things added quiet and small in scale. The difference is amazing and the expenditure has been very small.

Let's take a more complicated adjustment involving a family. You may be a family of five, with three children about to come into their teens, and have to change base in every way. The family used here had two boys and a girl. The father, who had a responsible position in a small city, was offered an excellent one that meant moving to a large city. They had to give up their comfortable four-bedroom home, with plenty of outside play space. It was impossible for them to find a suitable house and they were forced to move into an apartment with its combination of high cost and small space. They found a six-room apartment (it can be done, so don't despair), living room, dining room, kitchen, and three bedrooms, two of them quite small.

They felt that the move was permanent but also hoped to go back eventually to a house in some suburban area. Consequently, they did not want to eliminate articles they would need there, if they could help it. Obviously, the apartment could not take as much furniture as they had—or wanted to keep. So this was a time for serious evaluation. Each member of the family made his selection of his own things—subject to discussion and final approval. In the case of articles that require much space, unless they can be used, the question of expense as to storage vs. rebuying later must be considered. And since in this case they had no way of knowing how long the things would be stored, it was doubly difficult.

All of the outdoor equipment—lawn mower, gardening tools, etc., which were in good condition, plus some newly purchased iron furniture, were set aside for storage. There was every possibility that they would be needed again and that the storage would be less than the cost of new ones. The laundry equipment, on the other hand, had seen a lot of use, was in perfectly good condition but far from up-to-date, and they decided to sell that. The garage held various and sundry objects for use in the care of the car and, since one of the boys was very much interested in mechanical things, these were carefully sorted and one large box of the most essential set aside for storage.

Before the furniture was chosen for the new apartment, the family had several sessions together, figuring how the space could be best used for everyone. They had a small-scale floor plan in front of them and the children had measured the over-all dimensions of all the more important pieces of furniture and cut out plans of them to a larger scale. The father drew up the floor plan to the larger, easy-to-see scale and they pushed the furniture around, working out the arrangements that seemed most functional and attractive. This was fun for the children and also gave them a feeling of familiarity with the new place so that it never did seem strange to them when they finally settled there.

The living room of the apartment was of a good size—16′ x 24′—and the dining room adjoined it with double doors between that could be closed. The master bedroom was also a comfortable size, with its own bathroom. The two small bedrooms were connected by a bath. They were large enough to accommodate twin beds, with necessary tables, two chests each, and a chair—no more. If the children's rooms are too small for any activity, it may be a good idea to make the dining room into a general playroom for them—but retain a potential for dining space. This room will also provide the only spot for extra sleeping space.

The room was 13′ x 15′, a size which will probably take a rug from your house. They used their dining-room rug, an oriental with small allover pattern and narrow border, which almost filled the room, making it look larger. A very sturdy sofa covered with a durable fabric that could take hard use was against one wall: it could be made into a double bed. On another they had a drop-leaf table with two deep leaves which could comfortably seat ten when opened and easily seat the family with one leaf up. Both of these pieces came from their house. They were tempted to build bookcases in this room, but they had so many from their house that they were able to choose the ones that could most readily be adapted to the wall space. They used them over two matching chests which provided the drawer space the children needed for their play and school supplies. The side chairs were strong ones that the children used when they were working at the table—the only flat working surface in the room—and they also doubled as dining-room chairs. For extra chairs they had a set of folding ones which were both comfortable and sound. While this was not exactly a substitute for the space they had had (there is NO real substitute for space), it gave them what they basically needed both as a playroom and a dining room. The kitchen was large enough for a round table so they could eat breakfasts and lunches there, when they happened to be at home, which was infrequently. You can do a room of this kind so that when in order it will have the look of a well-used study and it can be made to look very acceptable when you are entertaining. Obviously, they could not do formal entertaining, but the table was perfect for the type of buffet they had, the extra room adding space to the living room.

The boys' bedroom had double-decker beds, brought with them, and the guest room twin beds were used in the girl's room, which became a guest room when there were guests—and she slept in the playroom. The parents had their own bedroom, which was inviolate, and since the children had a fair amount of space and privacy in their playroom, the setup made it possible for them to keep out of each other's hair. Even though the children had to play and study in the same place, they had their own bedrooms where they could go for privacy. The living room and master bedroom both took the furniture from the house as though it had been planned for them—even including the curtains. The family lived in the apartment for three years before they moved back into a house in the suburbs and it worked out so well that they were sorry to leave.

Or you may be a small family of three, coming from a town where you have had a small house to a large house in a city. In the move used, there were two outstandingly favorable aspects. The house this family moved into was a lovely one and the mother had real talent for making her home attractive on a small budget. This was fortunate, since it was a minister's family and there was not a great deal of money to do with. An added handicap in the decorating of a parsonage or rectory is the fact that it belongs somewhat to the congregation and the vestry, and there is usually a strong feeling against change. In this case, Mrs. R. was able to make her changes with patience, tact, and such a real feeling for the house that everyone approved.

The house they went into is a square brownstone, probably built in the middle of the nineteenth century. It has a hospitable center door, in a small entrance porch, and a wide hallway with a lovely curved stairway. On the right is the living room through a double opening and back of that the kitchen. On the left the hall opens into a charming sitting room with southern exposure, and behind that is a large dining room. Back of the hallway, between kitchen and dining room, is a large butler's pantry that has become a pleasant breakfast room. On the second floor are four bedrooms, a study, and two baths.

The architecture in the house is good but it had all been painted, including the walls, in dreary, drab colors which completely eliminated it as a decorative asset. Mrs. R. went quickly to work to correct that. She planned her colors very carefully, since all of the main downstairs rooms open off the hall and are seen very much together. She used a wallpaper in the hall with shades of soft blues and grays. For the living room she selected one of the greener grays in a fairly strong value. For the sitting room she chose a soft gray with a bluish cast and for the adjoining dining room a deeper tone of gray-blue.

In each room the architecture was picked out by painting it a lighter tone, including the chimney pieces in the living and dining rooms, adding considerably both to their character and the decorative effect. This color scheme kept the rooms appropriately subdued for a parsonage, but since the family is a gay and happy one, she used various shades of soft reds for her curtains, all of which she made herself. The reds added greatly to the warmth and friendliness of the rooms. She had wooden cornices cut, which the high ceilings could well take and which simplified both the making (less trouble with headings which are concealed) and the hanging of the curtains.

For her dining room, some twenty years earlier, she had chosen chairs made at that time, but reproductions of seventeenth-century English ones. She now proceeded to find some authentic pieces of the same period. This required time and thought and naturally involved some money. It was at about this time that Mrs. R. stumbled onto the auctions and it was this discovery that made it possible for her to complete the furnishing of her home as she wanted it, but had not been able to foresee with much hope. If you have the time and interest, auctions can be very rewarding. She found a beautiful refectory table and two sideboards, all of which are handsome and functional additions to her room. She bought one of the pieces, which has been recently valued at a very high figure, for under twenty dollars. The chairs have been kept and, used with red velvet cushions to match the curtains, which she made, they are sufficiently elegant for the rest of the room. The total effect is right.

Mrs. R.'s system, from the beginning, was to hunt until she found just what she wanted—no compromising. In the case of two pieces —a canopy four-post bed and a Sheraton cabinet, she started by paying five dollars to have them held, and then put aside a small amount each week for more than a year until she could go and claim them. This requires a co-operative and understanding dealer and she found him very helpful before she discovered the auctions. It is a well-known fact a dealer may give you credit but auctions require cash. She advises that you have a special fund into which you put money so it will be there when you happen on the thing you need at an auction. Keep lists of what you buy and where; certain things are more apt to show up at certain places. You can learn much about good design, woods, and in fact everything concerning furniture by these trips to the auction galleries.

Being a more than kindly soul, she often worries about the people who have had to sell their treasures, but the few times she has been able to find out the history, it hasn't been sad at all. In the case of a very beautiful and unusual secretary that she felt was a very special bargain she found that it had come from the apartment of two elderly ladies who had decided that they wanted a trip around the world and simply wanted to be foot-loose. They were apparently as happy to get rid of the piece as she was to have it and undoubtedly, if they had loved it, they would have felt grateful to know that she had it.

Over the years, through making her own mistakes, she has developed a number of practical rules which she recommends. Take your time about making all decisions in regard to what you really want, and allow the time to be spent living in the setup where the addition is to be used. Be careful not to order or buy anything in advance of a complete understanding of its need and use. Before she made this move she took several pieces of worn furniture to be upholstered locally. After the move they were all wrong and she decided never to do that again. This is a case where hindsight can be used and can do a good job and foresight may ruin it. Spend your money on a few good pieces, which key the rooms and make it possible to use simple and inexpensive furniture for the balance without spoiling the total effect. Her home, which is at the same time dignified and gracious and also completely comfortable and functional, attests to the successful use of her theories.

Or you may be a person with a family, in some branch of government service—the armed forces, the diplomatic or consular service, or any situation where there is a chance of being moved around or living in another country. There is no possibility of standardization for these moves and very few sound generalities can be offered because the fabulous variety of locality, kind of quarters, and living conditions simply do not permit it. After chatting with a few people who have had experience in living hither and yon, I'm going to summon my courage and offer a little advice.

It is a good idea to start with a little self-analysis and have the rest of the family do the same; you'll have to do it for the younger members of the family. Consider what is most important to you in your everyday living and on the basis of whatever this turns up, decide what is truly indispensable to you that may be impossible to get where you are going. In deciding what to take, remember that you are likely to grow to hate things that have to be packed and handled, and choose only those articles that you would be miserable without. If you are heat-conscious and feel wretched when you can't keep comfortably warm, then by all means take an electric pad. One person also took two old-fashioned kerosene heaters and not only never regretted it, but eventually felt that the stoves had literally saved lives. She tucked in three sheets—just in case—which turned out to be useful for lining her bedroom curtains. Material for the curtains was issued, but no lining. This was in Japan and the house was not insulated; the lined curtains were a real help in keeping the cold out on the window wall.

There are many objects that we take for granted and others that are simple to buy in this country, but not so elsewhere. Coat hangers are a good example: we have quantities of the wire ones, which are both inexpensive and easy to pack. We usually consider hangers indispensable, but they are apt to be difficult, if not impossible, to get in many countries. Bathroom scales are essential to some people and difficult to buy in most countries. This can be true of an electric iron—particularly if you have definite preferences, as we can have in this country. All wearable clothes that you have should be taken because the chances are that you will be gone long enough so they will be out-of-date, and if you do get through with them you can usually find someone who needs them. Special medicines and an extra pair of glasses and similar articles are on almost everyone's travel list but should be given extra consideration at this time.

Another person who went to Asia could not be convinced that servants, no matter how many, could completely replace certain of her devices. She took a small, apartment-size automatic washer and found it to be one of her indispensables. She had five servants, but in a brief time the two girls who were responsible for the laundry were able to do it entirely—and much cleaner than by hand—plus actually enjoying the work. The matter of sanitation can be a difficult one and even more so where small children are concerned. She found that her little machine simplified everything. For her kitchen she took her own dishwashing gear—nothing automatic—but things she could not buy there. With a dish rack and plenty of hot water you can teach your helpers to wash the dishes in such a way that they are really clean. We take this business of cleanliness much more for granted than people in other parts of the world and it is well to remember that.

A good idea is to take a pamphlet file; wherever you move, you will find that you can use and add to it. When a young wife had her house painted in the Orient she had no problems. She had colored photographs showing the way she wanted it done—color on a ceiling, in the closets, etc. She said that she never in the world could have convinced those painters that this was what she wanted—and got—if she hadn't shown them the pictures. While this is something few people would think of, it could be a helpful hint.

It is always smart to find out as much as you can about the place you are going so that you can have some practical notion of conditions—what is and isn't available. Once you get there, look around for the good things of the region and adjust to the life as it is being lived there. Don't waste any time wishing you were back in the good old U.S.A. because that time you waste could so well be spent in getting to know that part of the world, an opportunity that you have that many of us do not. When you are ready to come back, just remember—your house, stateside, can accommodate only a limited number of those brass trays that are so beautiful and such a good buy. And you can't be giving them away indiscriminately, so take it a little easy. You do know something of the life you will be leading when you get back, so stock up thoughtfully and with judgment.

6 A Reasonable Shore

Since a primary aim of this book is to encourage and help anyone sincerely interested in taste to develop assurance in his own, some further understanding of the elements of good taste is necessary. Let's explore the matter of taste and the evolution of its increasing importance in our present day.

A general interest in taste and a consciousness of its significance is a comparatively recent development. One reason for this is that during the seventeenth and eighteenth centuries, only people with money—a very small group—had time to give to the aesthetic matters through which one's taste can evolve. Although the political upheavals of the eighteenth century were the beginning of the recognition of the importance of the individual, to the great majority of people survival remained the basic urge and there was little time for anything not concerned with that. Even in our country, during the nineteenth century, the West was being settled and life was not only strenuous but extremely rugged.

Except for newly emerging families of great wealth, few people were at all interested in cultural things. This group had had no opportunity to understand such things, had no confidence in their own ideas, and in fact went so far as to admit that they themselves were totally lacking in taste. With no Americans designing for luxurious living, it was inevitable that they should turn to Europe for their backgrounds, which marks the beginning of the so-called antique business. There was nothing with any distinction whatsoever being designed in our own country at that time, and these people, whose wealth was such an overpowering thing, felt that the backgrounds which were satisfactorily elegant for the aristocracy of Europe could not fail to provide what they wanted.

Scientific, sociological, and tax changes during the present century have made this kind of living impossible and it is in the evolution of what has replaced it that we discover the new emphasis on taste. There are many contributing factors. Briefly, the complete breakdown of the remnant of class distinction that had survived as a carry-over among the naturalized Americans born in countries where it existed, plus the gradual automation that has given the average person so much morc leisure, brought a consciousness of "taste"—vague at first to be sure—to increasingly large numbers of people. The many academies and colleges established as fast as the new areas were settled, and the opportunity to travel abroad that came with the steamship, broadened the outlook of thousands plus the many who heard about it from them. All this happened gradually, but by the time we were well into this century the widened horizon had become accepted.

It remained for the adman to make a big thing of it and in the last twenty-five years the advertising business has had more influence on taste than any other institution in the records of history. The influence has been mixed. Advertising agencies are spending incredibly large sums to develop tastes. In the process they have contributed to popular knowledge of good taste. But their main motive is to sell, and often they tend to neglect the constructive aspect, as such. So, on the one hand we have the products that are promoted by advertisements almost completely unconcerned with any constructive aspect. The superficial, materialistic, and frequently artificial tastes that they stimulate in beguiling and superbly artful ways have contributed to or possibly coincided with a decadence in taste that sometimes seems to overbalance the tremendous over-all contribution made jointly by good design and good advertising. This tasteless kind of advertising must be eye- or ear-catching, spectacular, planned for high-pressure selling, totally unconcerned with sincerity. In the "olden days" the buyer was warned to beware. Now it is this kind of an advertiser you should be cautioned against. Think back over the past decades and consider, in retrospect, the variety of products that have been represented as the "final word." If you will pause a moment and take note of the conspicuous fact that many of these products have ultimately proved worthless, it will help you to resist high-pressure selling that claims to be the "answer" to all your needs.

On the other hand the real and constructive contribution good advertising has made has been colossal. Without the budget, the capable, vigorous activity, and the knack of gaining interest and readership that is characteristic of this profession, much that has been tremendously beneficial in this respect would never have been seen, let alone comprehended by the public. Advertising is, after all, intended to acquaint you with a product in such a way as to make you want to buy it. When you have a good product and advertising has been and is done honestly and artistically, as it so often is, it is close to being a real art. Certainly the level of taste in the better advertising is extremely high and frequently constructive. We owe much of our present standard of living to this often beautiful advertising, which, in addition to its own intrinsic contribution, makes possible the many handsome magazines available to us.

In company with the various kinds of showmanship—theaters, movies, opera, radio and TV—and all visual promotion, especially fashion and home, advertising in general has had a tremendous influence on taste and has both corrupted and hastened its development. There is, in the very theory of the advertising profession, danger of glorifying the superficial, a tendency to substitute know-how for knowing. Samuel Johnson has said, "The trade of advertising is now so near perfection that it is not easy to propose any improvement. But as every art ought to be exercised in due subordination to the public good, I cannot suppose it as a moral question to those masters of the public ear, whether they do not sometimes play too wantonly with our passions."

While advertising has been powerful in molding taste in general and in every department of daily living, we have had the editorial content of newspapers and magazines working effectively toward the forming of taste and toward a consciousness of its importance. Without the development of this consciousness, surely it would be an impossibly uphill project to improve general taste standards. They have unquestionably contributed greatly to these standards, which continue to rise and always with their assistance, cooperation, and, in fact, leadership. Although the great dailies across the country keep their editorial policy separate from products for which they accept advertising, not all newspapers can manage it. I was raised in a newspaper family and my father had ethical standards as high as any human being I have ever known. He would not accept advertising that did not meet with his standards (it once cost me a new bicycle). But understandably he felt that he should support the people who kept him going—his advertisers. In the decorating field there is likely to be, in some newspapers, a relationship between paid advertising space and editorial comment and such comment is usually not disparaging. Sometimes, in this process, bad design gets kindly editorial comment. The layman takes it at face value. This is a practice that is disappearing, and you can figure out for yourself whether or not you are being exposed to it.

The consumer who is hoping to learn from the various writings on the subject will find them in many places. In most daily newspapers there is a page each week devoted to home furnishings, and sometimes a daily column. The usefulness of these will vary. Often the genuine interest and sincerity with which these stories are done will give them value, so you be the judge. Screen all of this material thoughtfully. In most papers it will be good and also have the virtue of being practical for local conditions—the climate, general way of living, regional preferences, etc. Unless you find ideas that seem tailored for your purpose, just be sure to evaluate with special care. It is a safe bet that you will be offered a number of general rules. These should be disregarded in many instances, unless something seems to be the answer to your specific problem. There has been so much more generalization in this field than is valid that it usually should be viewed with suspicion. Avoid confusion by making use of this source only when it truly interests you and is directed toward your exact needs of the moment. Because there may be information that is good and useful for you, read it—and then try to consider it on a completely personal basis. If it conflicts with opinions that you have carefully and thoughtfully developed, forget it. The chances are that your own ideas are better for you. Anyway in the process of adjustment to these conflicting ones, confusion will be inevitable.

The less expensive shelter magazines have been improving steadily, and continue to do so, but are far from infallible. The same criterion should be applied to them as to the newspapers. They will also have more pictures and many constructive features. You should be especially careful in evaluating for yourself stories on homes that have some special angle. Very often there is something valuable to be learned from that part of the story, while the taste level of the rest of the house may not be so high. Use discrimination between the specific point of the story, which is probably good, and the incidental part, which may be less so. Since your taste is what we are concerned with, don't fool around with anything that doesn't appeal strongly to you. Then apply the few simple rules in Chapter 2.

The same kind of discrimination should be accorded the many new magazines distributed only through the supermarkets. I believe that one of their most rewarding features is the articles which give interesting and practical instructions for doing or making things yourself. For those who are blessed with this ability these articles can be of real assistance. But beware of being inspired to make pieces of gadgety junk that will be no asset to any home. Think carefully and be sure that whatever you turn out will have something of a professional look and will definitely contribute to that certain feeling that you aspire to in your home.

The third group are the old stand-bys, the women's magazines. The service they have dispensed over the years and the meticulous care with which they have built up their machinery for providing it is, like the fine advertising, a public service that few of the people who make use of it could otherwise afford. It has helped them in countless ways—to understand household management, raise their standards of living without increased spending, and many others. The Good Housekeeping Institute, one of the oldest and best-known organizations set up for testing for the benefit of the public, is an amazing place—operated as meticulously as any scientific laboratory. Its Consumers' Guaranty has been an incomparable boon to the public for many years. More recently, another helpful and practical testing bureau has been set up by *McCall's* magazine. Their service involves not only the testing of a product, but its actual use, over a period of time, under normal household conditions. Articles passing this test are given their "Use-tested Tag." These magazines have a high standard and the people who run the various departments have specialized in each field. These services are solid, sensibly geared to the income bracket of their subscribers, and while they, also, should be mulled over and permitted to influence *your* opinions only if they seem at home there, they are both reliable and helpful.

The last group, the so-called shelter or home-furnishing magazines have also done their part, and a very substantial one, in both educating and improving tastes and making life more comfortable. The fact that they can produce for the reader such a handsome and expensive magazine at a price he can afford is due to the advertisers who buy their advertising space. And nothing is spared to produce an extremely good-looking publication, put together with intelligence and taste. They are edited by people who are specialists and usually experts.

These are the most powerful and obvious influences on taste in the field of interior design. The contradictions or inconsistencies in some of this material—both promotional and editorial—have to some degree confused the average reader. How many people do you know who have built a house in the past decade—starting out hopefully and ending up broke and disillusioned? It certainly has happened among people I know and it is not necessary.

You should be sure that you understand just what you want in your home, just what you are getting into in its planning, and just exactly how that planning can result in the thing you want and expect. It is terribly expensive and tragically unrewarding to go all-out on your home without a thorough and complete understanding of what and how and, when you don't know, why. You must make it your business to understand. When the house is built and you discover that it is not for your way of living, it is too late.

The bitter "modern vs. traditional" controversy has further added to the difficulty. It is covered in the next chapter, but since so much editorial space has been given to the modernist point of view, many people feel like outcasts if they don't wholly subscribe to it. One of the things that puzzle them is the complete repudiation of the past in so much of this writing.

In the fields of music, fine arts, and literature, there has been no such general denial of the worth of the contribution of the past. The most modern of composers, whose music may be understood (if at all) only by the esoteric few, still study Bach and find him a gold mine of knowledge that they are able to use. The more recent the composer, usually, the greater the disagreement concerning his value, but on the whole the same great composers are revered by the contemporary student of music. This is also true in painting and sculpture, and it is a rare occasion, indeed, when you hear some struggling young painter or sculptor speak with scorn of Leonardo or Bellini or Donatello. And how many modern writers have crossed Shakespeare off their lists?

There is controversy in these fields, but it is more tolerant and less emotional and certainly more constructive. Nor is it quite as universal, since, in varying degrees, design, which is concerned with the matter of living, interests almost everyone alive.

There is another strong force that has added to the complication —the current overemphasis on function. Function is absolutely basic and there can be no question of its importance and necessity. But it is important not as an end in itself but only as the beginning of a lovely, practical home. And as long as people are people, once function is taken care of, is there any reason why they can't have some fun and at the same time satisfy their own aesthetic sense? I heard Sir Hugh Casson, one of England's outstanding architects, give a delightful talk to a group of students and was struck by his fine combination of the practical with the aesthetic. Shortly after, I saw an account of an interview with him in *The New Yorker* and highly approved of his remarks. "I suppose I'm not wholly committed to the functionalist ideal . . . When it comes to townscape I like the sense of happy accidents that have taken place over the years, and I'm not above inventing them. I see nothing immoral in providing architectural pleasures—unexpected vistas, the surprise of coming on a square, a fountain—that have nothing to do with efficiency. I strongly dislike the image of a city as a sort of patient with a dozen doctors hovering over him, fussily making sure that his internal organs are all in order. One ought to be able to assume that the internal organs of a city—its power, its water, its sewers—are in order and go on from there to make it beautiful or exciting—or at any rate interesting."

I suppose this American overemphasis on "function" is tied up with our tragic dependence, for contentment, on our material possessions. When I returned from a several months' stay in Europe recently I was once again overwhelmed by the basic difference in our way of living. It seems to me that they don't push nearly as hard as we do and so have time to enjoy as they go whatever rewards they may earn. Their sense of values can't be as materialistic as our own because it is impossible for them to get all that we have in the way of conveniences and automatic appliances. So, they depend for their happiness on other things and in spite of their lack of automatic facilities they seem happier and better able to find satisfaction and security within themselves than we, with our creature comforts and hustle and bustle. Although the highways of Europe are becoming more and more crowded, it is certainly true that the average family, there, doesn't dissipate an unreasonable amount of its budget on a means of transportation, as we are inclined to do. Many families have no car and those who do usually have smaller ones that are economical to operate. This leaves more of everything for the home—more money to spend and more time to enjoy it. Perhaps we would do well to give some thought to the knack with which so many European families balance their spending in the most rewarding way.

In the last act of *The Tempest*, Prospero says, "Their understanding begins to swell; and the approaching tide will shortly fill the reasonable shores . . ." For the vast number of people who have become confused and uncertain as a result of modern sales promotion and style controversy, there must be a way through to an understanding that is reasonable. It seems inconceivable that in this country of practical souls, the reasonable shore of intelligent and constructive thought in the field of design has been left high and dry. If you will learn to make your own selections on the basis of established principles, it will help the situation immeasurably. More important, you'll be happier too.

7

Never Mind What Style— Just Have It Right for You

In interior design the style currently referred to as modern is comparatively new. Interior designers made the break with the tradition of the past after it had been made by the architects. Since architecture, as a profession, is much older than the relatively recent one of interior design, this is logical. However, in order to understand the point of view of the modernist, it is necessary to understand something about the revolution in the field of architecture that has taken place during the past century. This change has been a significant one and the best way to follow what has been happening is to apply some serious thought to comprehending the practical and philosophical convictions of a few of the best-known exponents.

In the controversy between the modernist and the traditionalist, the extreme conservatives and the violent liberals usually make the most noise. Emerson has said that "The castle which conservatism is set to defend is the actual state of things, good and bad." But if we are to be practical, who is the judge of what is good and bad? On the outside edge of the conflict there are the reactionary conservatives at one end and, on the other, the modernists bent on change simply for the sake of change. If we examine the better and less extreme exponents of both sides, perhaps we can find a way through the confusion which will be of real help in evaluating the work of the many sound and sincere designers of all styles who have been steadily at work throughout the fracas.

First, let us be definite as to what we mean by the two words—modern and traditional. The lack of agreement as to the meaning of "modern" has caused unnecessary confusion. Here, it refers to architecture and furnishings based on a new concept of design, construction, and materials not necessarily related to anything produced in the past. Traditional interiors are based on architecture of the past, with suitable furniture, not necessarily of the same period. The home which I call contemporary is not involved in this aspect of the dispute because it is simply a home of today, belonging to this time and perfectly adapted to it; it can be partially modern, or traditional, or is very likely to have a combination of both. These definitions may seem arbitrary, but for the sake of clarity and consistency definitions are essential.

So, we start with modern architecture, around which the hottest and most controversial arguments have centered. There are many hundreds of fine architects who are doing a capable job of creating a new type of home for the family of today—especially in this country, where there is more of most everything—particularly money and space. There are hundreds more who are simply cashing in on the need and are turning out houses, whether with modern or traditional trappings, that are in every way a disgrace to their profession, for one purpose only—to make money. Behind both of these groups are the pioneers in modern architecture and it is among them that we look for our modern point of view.

In this connection, the first name that comes to mind is surely Frank Lloyd Wright, whom we hear a great deal about, not only because he was the first American innovator in the field of architecture, but also because he has a terrific capacity for making himself heard. Wright feels that sincere design, in the past, ended with Gothic architecture. He accuses the architects of the Renaissance of being "operators" who arranged the classic orders not, as they should, in a natural way but according to their own tastes, giving an unjustified emphasis to the front or a façade of a building which was a design in itself with no relationship to the inside. His theory is that organic architecture is the only right answer and he describes it: "Organic building is natural building—construction proceeding from the nature of a planned or organized inside to a consistent outside. The space to be lived in is now the human reality of the building and in terms of space we find the new forms we seek." What this means in terms of his architecture is that space becomes the basic element in the designing of any building. The exterior forms, which enclose the space, are incidental to it. He has rebelled against boxlike rooms and has broken through walls, arranging the rooms of his houses in a new way—completely unorthodox to traditionalists. His houses usually feature one of his creations—the picture window—which brings the outside in and to some extent lets the inside out. His picture windows are intended to be used where there is a view; and he integrates his structures with the landscape, designing each house individually to fit the site as well as the needs of the owner. The character of the house must begin with and be determined by the kind of land on which it is to be built. Wright tends toward horizontal lines parallel to the landscape and uses natural materials so that his houses seem to melt into their background. As anyone who has seen his houses knows, the tendency is for the viewer to see the entire composition—house and background or site—instead of noticing the building alone.

I visited his first prefabricated house in Madison, Wisconsin, and after a study of the man and his work I truly anticipated seeing it. But I found it a disappointment and distinctly felt that it was not much house for $34,000, plus quite a number of essential extras. As usual, it is nicely situated and Mr. Wright specifies that it should be built on a site of at least one acre. In the process of building, it is suggested that he come and have a look and when it is done he will come (these trips of course at the buyer's expense) and install his famous "red block" if it warrants his approval. As for the house itself, it seems to me to give a minimum of space for the investment. The living room is two steps below the entrance, for no observable reason—which takes away a sizable piece of floor space in a very expensive manner. There are three bedrooms, none of them large, with their closet space further cutting down on their size. Two of them have windows on one side only and all have a thin type of accordion door that ensures very little privacy. One outside wall of approximately thirty-five feet is given over entirely to the bedroom hall. Calling it a gallery and placing windows along its entire length does not cancel the fact that it is very expensive space for a passageway. The dining area in the living room seemed inflexible to me; and as for the family, when they eat in the kitchen they unsociably face the wall—except for one lucky soul who can look out the single window in that area. There is no garage, only a carport (Madison is cold and often snowy in the winter), and a very small amount of storage space. I find these features questionable in view of the $34,000-plus price tag involved. He is also working on some prefabs with a slightly lower price level.

His publicity has been so overwhelming that too many people feel an inadequacy in themselves if they don't like his houses. Since he is not a tolerant person and sees little good in any opinion that disagrees with his own, this is pure foolishness. There are large numbers of people who simply do not want to live as his houses decree —and they do dictate a certain way of living. There is a lack of privacy (bedroom walls of rough planks stopping below the ceiling), a dependency on a green thumb (planters as part of basic decorative design), and interior use of concrete and stone, not acceptable to some people. Mr. Wright has designed many beautiful homes (none of them inexpensive), and after seeing several with a considerable amount of variation I have yet to see the one where I would want to live. Perhaps I may have something in common with the critic who, after seeing an exhibition of Wright's work, quipped, "I'd rather be Wright than be resident."

Mr. Wright is too prone to "operate" on the basis of his own ideas—exactly as he accuses the Renaissance architects of doing on theirs. In the process he ignores a variety and honest difference of opinion on this entire subject. There are millions of intelligent people who have other ideas as to the way they want to live, and are entitled to them. It is too bad that he doesn't permit himself to remain a great person in the minds of the public by stepping out of the limelight while the greatness is what they will remember. It is sad to pick up a Sunday paper and see, casually, in a department store advertisement, "Frank Lloyd Wright—40% to 70% off." This, of course, referred to his unsuccessful furniture designs. But it also points up the fact that he is far from infallible. His opinions are not what you should concern yourself with; forget them and evaluate his architecture purely on the basis of your own reactions to it.

The other best-known names of the pioneering days can be grouped under the "International Style," sponsored and championed in this country by the Museum of Modern Art. They are men who first attracted attention in Europe. Mies Van der Rohe came from Germany, and in 1938 became director of architecture at what is now called the Illinois Institute of Technology. Although the campus there is probably his most important work in this country, he is better known for the glass apartment house on Michigan Avenue in Chicago. His personal motto, as well as his whole theory of design, has always been "less is more"—and everything he does illustrates this desperately stark simplicity. Says Mies, "We refuse to recognize problems of form, but only problems of building. Form is not the aim of our work, but only the result. Form, by itself, does not exist. Form as an aim is formalism and that we reject." Walter Gropius, for many years chairman of the Department of Architecture at Harvard, is founder of the school in Germany known as the Bauhaus. He calls it "the yeast of the modern art movement." His aim was to help the artist or designer to recover the feeling of execution as an important part of his task—"the fine old sense of design and execution being one." Charles Édouard Jeanneret-Gris, better known as Le Corbusier, is represented directly in this country only as one of the designers of the United Nations buildings, but his influence has been strongly felt. He has talked and written a great deal, but in such irrelevant generalities that finding a remark containing an explicit idea is difficult—it all sounds like double talk. Where ideas can be picked out, they seem more concerned with imposing arbitrary rules of life than interpreting architectural design in understandably human terms. In contrast to Wright, who thinks in terms of Nature (his capital), Le Corbusier's work is deliberately man-made. He is the person who first called the home a "machine for living." His spectacularly publicized apartment house on stilts, in Marseille, has not proven to be very constructive—having provided very expensive and badly disposed living space with a minimum of privacy. An American who lived in one of his houses said, "He is a functionalist who seems to function differently from the rest of us."

On the style, I quote Philip C. Johnson, a prominent American architect who has written and spoken frequently about it, helping to make it and its results understood in this country. "This international order was based on a new appreciation of the technical and structural inventions of the previous century. Its aesthetic characteristics are: 1. the regularity of skeleton structure as an ordering force in place of axial symmetry; 2. the treatment of exteriors as weightless non-supporting skins rather than as heavy solids obedient to gravity; 3. the use of color and structural detail in place of applied ornament."

This is in complete contrast to the type of houses being built in this country at the time the style was introduced. Most important to our houses were the strong exteriors, solidly placed on the ground, doors and windows usually symmetrically placed, and often some kind of applied, decorative detail.

The International Style appears to be autocratic; there is in it a strong tendency to ignore the human element—which Heaven knows we would all like to do at times. But we can't overlook the fact that it is not only a wonderfully persistent element but the eternal source, through imagination, of a variety of joyous and practical creativity not possible under such restrictions.

Who (or what) but a human being, as seen in a timely cartoon, would have the courage and enterprise to rush out of his safely protected hut and kick a space rocket to get it off the ground? No one but just us humans, and let's not concentrate on subjection of this precious quality or lose sight of it in the designing of our homes, which, for most of us, are much more than "machines for living."

There are a number of important modern architects—some students of these men and many who are not—such names as Neutra, Breuer, Saarinen, and others who have made a real contribution in this field. They have much in common and in general their principles are similar to those just discussed. Among them, they have had a tremendous influence on building today—in every phase. The honest and capable modernists have both accomplished much and contributed greatly to the evolution of design. But there has been a strong proclivity toward an absolutism in their thinking that seems to say that *theirs* is the only right design—and for everyone—with insufficient regard for individual reactions. On the whole they have repudiated the past and since most of the architects doing the more spectacular, large new buildings come from this school of thought, the majority of these buildings are in this style. Before we hastily tear down everything that has been considered good in the past, depriving us of any further opportunity to see what was good about it, perhaps we should take a little more time to scrutinize the subject. I think that the potential results of this movement, which seems to be surging unchecked toward a fearful conformity, should be evaluated with painful care. It is both powerful and potent, and since architecture, in the past, has led the way, this trend toward an antihuman standardization will surely be reflected more and more in our homes—whether we like it or not.

In all of our large cities today many new buildings are going up. A few good modern buildings, especially as planned together, can be an asset. The problem, as it is illustrated in New York, has not been duplicated elsewhere. With the particular layout of Manhattan Island there are only a few important avenues, running parallel for a considerable distance, north and south. This, plus a kind of sectional activity, has caused a concentration of such buildings, not found in other large cities. Today there is a frantic amount of building going on. Anyone who cherishes a sense of continuity is purely out of luck. The scene changes so fast that you can't even leave for a week and come back to find it the same. And this is no slight change that is taking place. On Park Avenue entire blocks have disappeared to be replaced by shining new ones. They are all office buildings—most of them replacing apartment houses. Structurally they conform in most ways to our definition of the International Style, being skeletons of a light framework, with exteriors of seemingly weightless, nonsupporting skins, generally known as curtain walls. The exteriors make more use of glass and aluminum than any other materials, but there is still a goodly amount of brick and some marble being used.

Individually, many of the buildings are handsome and actually there is variation in their design. Collectively, they are monotonous and at the rate they are going up, another year or two will see a solid row on both sides of the avenue. In spite of much basic good design, they already seem to lack character, and the more of them one sees together, the more each loses its identity. Beauty has been defined as "the perfection of form resulting from the harmonious combinations of diverse elements in unity" or, more simply, the quality of harmonious relationships. There is no formula for it and since the eye of the beholder is the medium of interpretation, no two people will react exactly the same. According to this definition, these modern buildings fulfill the requirements. But, if this is the case, is beauty enough? I doubt if the average human being will be satisfied with the coldly perfect proportion and the standardization accentuated by so many of them together. I believe it is possible and practical to combine both fine proportion and utilization of beautiful materials with character-giving qualities.

People, in honesty, do prefer character, and the many I have listened to on this subject generally not only dislike this kind of conformity but fear its influence on their homes. Some of them have been battered into acceptance on the basis of fulfillment from a functional angle. But is there complete function, or has the fearfully efficient appearance been partly responsible for this feeling? It is probably too soon to be sure. But even if there is, the fact does remain that there can be an overemphasis on automation and function, and it leaves one helpless when it backfires. Fortunately, common sense is a human quality that persists, and a young couple I know had an experience which illustrates how it can come to the rescue. They lived in an apartment which had its own thermostat, presumably helpfully connected to an oil burner, which was supposed to control their temperature. The little gimmick was that the thermostat could not be set above 70 degrees; when cold weather set in, it turned out that the inside wall, where it was located, controlled its reading instead of the temperature in the room—which had northern exposure. When the living room was actually 62 or so degrees the thermostat cheerfully recorded 70. They finally conceived the idea of using ice cubes to convince it that the room was really cold and although this was a lot of bother, it did work, and they managed to get through the winter, having made a decision to move before cold weather set in again. This is one of thousands of such incidents of automatic backfire. Anyone who has been forced to drive several miles in a torrential rain with car windows down because there was no manual control is bound to feel sympathetic on the subject.

Even if these buildings can be indisputably functional, it is also their responsibility to provide true visual satisfaction. They no doubt do for some persons, but for others they do not and many people find the conformity confusing. I wonder just what percentage of tourists, taking that particular "Grand Tour" for the first time, can remember which is which after they get home—with the possible exception of those set back from the street—notably the first green glass one and the one made of bronze and glass. There is so little to give them identity—a minimum of individuality and no clue to their scale. Ornament, *as part of their design*, would help to provide both, and would certainly contribute to the pleasure of the viewer. The present need for right decorative design to counteract the frightening conformity has never been greater. This is increasingly true of the other avenues, adding just that much faster to the cumulative effect. There is certainly, here, no possibility of the "happy accident" mentioned by Sir Hugh Casson. The dizzying effect, as they repeatedly mirror each other in shimmering, drunken reflections, adds to the accumulation and also spoils the pleasure one used to get in walking down the avenue.

There is also the attempt to be original simply to attract attention and unfortunately designers of homes are quick to follow along. The building which turns an honest material such as aluminum into gold is an example of this; it is pure bogus.

The question has been posed: Are they any worse than those they replace? There should be no such question—they must be better. These are more than a few new buildings; they are leading the way. In the trial and error of pioneering there is certain to be a variety of errors. Isn't it now time for us to start evaluating and make an earnest effort to sort out the sound design? In too many of these buildings, the monotony, the obvious limitation and consequent copying of design is becoming apparent to more and more interested persons. Could these severe, somehow patronizingly inhuman, square-topped buildings, so rapidly filling the spaces made by recent demolitions, be the ones referred to by Frederick Mortimer Clapp in his *Cadenza in C Minor?*

Yet even now, moved by some relentless summons,
Fallacious skyscrapers rise
As if just by rising they could revivify
An exorable sky,
They that hint at no beyondness in existence.

In his introduction to *Built in U.S.A., Post War Architecture,* Henry-Russell Hitchcock says, "Today there is no further need to underline the obvious fact that what used to be called 'traditional' architecture is dead if not buried." I am convinced that this is a much stronger generalization than the situation justifies and that the "whole-hog" movement toward modern and what has been termed organic design has started a reaction in the opposite direction, which is the pattern of the past.

In an early Good Design contest for furniture, the Museum of Modern Art defined organic design: "A design may be called organic when there is a harmonious organization of the parts within the whole, according to structure, material and purpose. Within this definition there can be no vain ornamentation or superfluity, but the part of beauty is none-the-less great—an ideal choice of material in visual refinement, and in the rational elegance of things intended for us."

Most of the prize-winning articles in this Good Design contest have been austere in their interpretation of modern. This has prompted me to delve into the meaning of "organic design." I find that the expression, as it may refer to a specific concept in this field seems to mean different things to different persons. As previously indicated, Frank Lloyd Wright has given one definition, the Museum of Modern Art another—and depending on your own understanding of "organic," you can figure out your own. Most simply stated, it refers to any design that evolves and is interrelated in a manner similar to that of a living organism. To be organic in this sense, a design possesses a co-ordination, an interdependence and logical relationship of parts conforming to our earlier definition of "unity." Such a design cannot be embellished for superficial reasons, nor in any arbitrary way. But this does not mean that appropriate decoration is forbidden. It must be achieved in a sound and aesthetic way so as to give pleasure and satisfaction that can be humanly understood. Actually, "organic design" is nothing new, but simply a fresh recognition of the quality that has been responsible for the best of our cultural inheritance.

Perhaps an indication of a change in the acceptance of this definition that somehow turns its back on us as human beings is a show since organized for the Museum of Modern Art by Mr. Hitchcock. The work in this exhibition could not be called traditional, but it departed even further from the standards of their definition of organic design. This show exhibited the work of Antoni Gaudi, a Spanish architect, and my own feelings are perfectly expressed by the well-known art critic, Emily Genauer. She refers to the architect's work as "melting frozen custards, nightmares in a hall of distorting mirrors, Disneyland at its dizziest, a mélange of masonry and metal shapes (all curves—Gaudi abhorred straight lines) that look as though they had been chewed up and spit out." And she adds, "But if the museum, in showing his work, helps them [architects] to recognize how much room there must be for fantasy, virtuosity and imaginative play [remembering our human needs] in architecture, gives them courage to break away from the terrible standardization that is blighting our cities, it will have made a great contribution."

Among the houses that illustrate this kind of design, probably one of the best known is the glass house built by Philip Johnson at New Canaan, Connecticut. The house has been seen in many magazines as well as frequently opened to the public on tours of houses. The exterior walls are of glass, with a minimum of interior solid wall to take care of essential privacy. There have been other similar houses, and among them some incidents of dissatisfaction with this way of living. Since Mr. Johnson designed his own house, he surely knew what he wanted and as far as I know is satisfied. But this kind of house represents a basic departure from accepted and familiar ideas where living is concerned. It is possible that some prospective home builders are not able to visualize accurately (it is hard to do), and the house they get is not what they had anticipated.

Anyone who proposes to plan for this type of living—and don't forget that it does involve just that—must take some time to consider what it entails. As I walked past the Seagram Building on an evening after the lights were on, I was disturbed by all of the "office-keeping" furnishings and equipment so plainly visible from the street, so that, at close range, the over-all effect of glass and bronze is completely destroyed. In a glass house there is no possibility of hurriedly pushing out of sight some unsightly pile that your child (or perhaps you yourself) has left in the middle of the room; there is no place where it won't be visible. This is one of countless occasions where concealed space can seem indispensable —and actually there is no real substitute for it.

A good designer must be creative, but this does not necessarily mean rejecting the knowledge of the past. Learning from the past does not have to involve copying. The sensing and understanding of its fundamental qualities through practice and experience can become an inspired and reliable guide to pure good design. The organic designers do not accept form in the sense that the antique man did, who considered it a basic element, but it hasn't disappeared from the vocabulary of design and probably won't. Why should we be wasteful and discard the wisdom gathered through the ages by our forebears, who were striving and coping with many of the same problems that we have today? Bernard Berenson, in his book *Seeing and Knowing,* observes from a uniquely objective spot that "It is in our own day that for the first time in history a long-accepted classical tradition, with all of its invaluable conventions, has been wantonly, jeeringly thrown away." Can't we be contemporary in our outlook and still take advantage of our heritage? This does not mean that we are not modern—only that we choose to discriminate for ourselves as to what is best for us.

Although it is generally accepted that design reflects the age during which it evolves, does this mean that in this technological, scientific, and space-conscious world of ours the so-called modern home is best for everyone? Aren't the individuals who are to live in these homes the ones best equipped to make that choice? They should know what they may have so they can make a choice—but let them choose. And there are other things to be considered. In the past the pace was sufficiently less hectic for people to give more time to the simple matter of living, and by that I do not mean the mechanics of living but the aesthetic, social, and intellectual aspects. In the eighteenth century, since there were no automatic aids to labor, everything was done in a much more leisurely manner and the result was a real interest in the development of a gracious way of living. It is not necessary to condone the accompanying social evils of the time to realize that because of the lack of emphasis on industry, science, etc., the business of nice living was given serious attention and became a fine and highly specialized art. Perhaps it is possible for people of our time to become fed up with the super-severe, super-automatic and sometimes soulless modern home and feel happier in one of another period. If the designs of some earlier period happen to please you and fit the way you want to live, are they actually less suitable because they did not evolve during the present? It surely should be your personal decision, and one that each family should make for itself on the basis of its own knowledge and feelings and not the opinions of someone else, no matter how brilliant and well informed that person may be.

So what about the statistically larger number of people who prefer not to live in a house evolving from abstract theory which frequently does not adjust to the requirements of comfortable and diversified living? They are not heard from so often, as is usually the case with those who have found the thing that gives them satisfaction—probably because they are too busy enjoying it. But they do have a valid point of view and occasionally express it. The celebration of the sixtieth anniversary of the Cooper Union Museum for the Arts of Decoration seemed to me to reaffirm the use and importance of the past in the field of design—an affirmation underlined by the museum's more recent showing of the ceramics of Pablo Picasso, which are so brilliant a demonstration of the persistence of fundamental principles of ceramic design.

The avowed purpose of this museum, when it was started, was not only aesthetic but practical and human: the assembling of objects which possessed beauty and use together. They were objects which had, as August Heckscher observed, quoting Arthur Symons, "a quiet undefeatable existence as beautiful things, made for use and perfectly adapted to their use." It was called a modern museum for two reasons: it was available to the public for looking and learning, and in the new machine age the relationship between art and industry was featured—and not to belittle the machine. Calvin S. Hathaway, director of the museum, gives its purpose "its aim of being useful in raising the level of design of the objects that furnish and adorn daily living . . . often enough it happens that objects in the collection admired in one context by an earlier generation develop other and equally valuable lessons for our own quite different day."

The last statement is a particularly significant one and the clue to the whole matter. Nothing could be quite as absolute as the modernists would have us think, because it is contrary to human nature—people just don't operate that way. What they like and want one decade is not what they choose the next. V. Sackville-West, in discussing the development of the country house in England, says, "The inside has 'grown' in the same way as the outside. There is no question of a 'period' room . . . Every owner acquired furniture . . . as the taste and fashion of his age suggested. Sometimes the taste of his age was 'good,' sometimes 'bad'; there is no

Absolute in such matters. Our appreciation depends on the taste and fashion of our own immediate age. We may esteem one style and condemn another. The next generation may reverse all our ideas." Design, through the centuries, has followed a pattern of change. Whenever a style becomes oversimplified or too severe there is a reaction toward more and eventually richer ornament and decoration, until it becomes overdone and then it turns again toward simplicity.

Certain things may remain constant, but the elusiveness and unpredictability of the reactions of human beings to design will always be with us. The environment that we choose as our background is the direct result of our previous environment and our own individuality—if we have a free choice. The effect of environment is, and always will be, one of the strongest and most scientific of the educational factors of a generation. It is with the functional and artistic phases of the background that we are concerned here, and they are bound to be a very basic component of environment. If we will take time to realize the psychological effect which the physical background has on the atmosphere of the home, we comprehend its importance. Here is the human element again, for one individual may react to the same environment in an entirely different way than another. This is an absolute truth and even a totalitarian system could not alter this, no matter what leveling restrictions they used.

An unwholesome, superficial, and high-pressure influence which must be included in this picture has made use of human vulnerability in an attempt to build up an inclination toward an adulation and a blind following of names that have been made important—or at any rate well known—through superficial means. This is done usually by people who care little for taste or discrimination, but are concerned only with recognition and prestige. The result has been a market for a kind of design that is shoddy and vapid, but a market too large to be ignored. The consumer who chooses what he buys to impress his acquaintances and prove his own status has been helped by a multitude who are only too willing to sell him whatever he wants as well as those always ready to tell him what he ought to want. In this kind of merchandise taste is completely incidental, since the idea is to impress with an expensive-looking or merely ostentatious article. Unfortunately, our automobile design has fallen into this sad state. It is easy to identify—the "biggest, best, or newest"—and is always referred to in superlatives. You can feel very sad when you pay a huge price for the very, very "biggest" and just six blocks away (maybe closer), if you can believe what you read, you run smack into it—and yours isn't the biggest at all.

But if the question arises as to whether or not it is better for people to be told what is best for them—if they haven't the ability to decide soundly for themselves, I believe the answer is no. They should go ahead and learn for themselves, even at the cost of their own mistakes. I certainly found myself rocked back on my heels by two statements in a recent issue of *Harper's Magazine*. "Doing one's best is not quite enough for the architect. This is especially true *if the public is free to have personal opinions about what is best* . . . Perhaps the most difficult challenge the architect has to meet in America is the feeling that in a democracy, every man's taste should have somewhat equal weight." As a decorator, I do realize what an architect can be up against when he is sincerely trying to do what his knowledge and experience suggests is best for his client, who sometimes hasn't the ability to decide. But the sad fact is that too many times an architect gives his client what he wants him to have, and if a person can't have an opinion about the house he is to live in, it has come to a pretty pass. Someone who built a very modern house a few years ago commented that he thought there should be two architects for each house—one to do the design that shows and another to make it functional. He had a hassle with his architect when he insisted on a garage where the architect had planned open space. Considering that it was the only space for a garage, that the house is closed a good part of the year, used only for weekends and in the summer, it is hardly functional without lockable storage space for lawn mower, tools, fuel, furnace, and other equipment. The owner won, but at the cost of unjustified worry. He had a very expensive architect and should not have been put in such a position. People go to architects as they do to doctors, because they need the help of a specialist. But the parallel stops there because few of them know much about the science of medicine, but most of them know a lot about the way they want to live.

In a recent article, Dorothy Thompson asks, "Is There a Right to Bad Taste?" It is a good question and I would answer it yes, although I certainly feel that there are few people, if any, who are not happier living with good taste. What I think she means is that everyone should be allowed to live in the way that suits him—and I agree. When anyone goes to an architect or a decorator for help, that person should use his training to give the client just that, to the best of his knowledge. Miss Thompson feels that architects (and I'm sure this is also meant for decorators) want to remodel your life, your habits, your country, your nature and your domestics. This would be quite a project and I think she overestimates the time and/or interest of the person who is being paid to do the job. But, too often, in the flush of "getting things done" the person willingly lets the architect or decorator have his own way and later regrets it. An ethical decorator will guard against such hasty decisions because he is more likely than the client to know when decisions are being made too hastily.

There is something to be said for any good style, and in this connection let's be sure what we mean by style. It is a true expression of a people and its times, whether they be Egyptian or French Empire. I am not referring to fashion, which is transitory and apt to be capricious. If it has a sound foundation, it becomes a style. One family may like and live happily with Early American and why not, if they like it? It is friendly, warm, and easy to live with. Much of the furniture of the period was made by artisans who planned both carefully and practically and took great pride in their work. There is no reason why a house of this design can't be successfully adapted to the way we live today. It was designed for basic living and well designed. Another family may choose a Victorian house—or they may have had to take it and make the best of it. According to John Maass, in his *View of Victorian America* the houses were right for the times and, instead of being imitators, the "builders attacked each new problem in a spirit of vigorous experimentation. Even their gallant failures have the merit of individuality." In our cramped, space-limited world, I have seen several families joyfully accept the drawbacks, being sufficiently rewarded by the space and character of their Victorian houses.

Or another family chooses an eighteenth-century house, French or English, elegant or provincial—it doesn't matter. If they like it and like living in it, it is best for them. There is something to be said for the feeling of security that a quiet and sound background—time-tried and part of the heritage of the past—can give us in these violently changing times.

If it is modern that you like, you should feel equally free to have that. There are thousands of beautiful modern houses across the country and if you do like the style, the chances are that you are familiar with this kind of design. But you should realize that the apparent simplicity does not mean that it is inexpensive. So choose your style, but remember that the style you choose is not nearly as important as the way you handle it. After you make your selection, on the basis of your knowledge and its personal appeal to you, then go all-out and see that it is as attractive and functional as possible.

Among the decorators and designers who have been successful in combining good design of all times are William Pahlmann and Edward Wormley. In his excellent book, *The Pahlmann Book of Interior Design*, Mr. Pahlmann says, "To me the spirit of living today, and the spirit of design today, is a judicious combination of the old and the new . . . The way you combine the elements of the past and the present—using the great heritage of excellent design to dignify and dramatize the clean, open spaces, the functional perfection, the casual ease and the wonderful convenience that our century has contributed—is the test of style." Mr. Wormley has been designing modern furniture for many years and using it successfully in a variety of backgrounds with fine furniture and accessories from all periods. There are many decorators who feel at home in any style—as long as they are working with good design.

It is the extremists you must recognize—those whose generalities are uttered as final authority. You must try to understand what all sincere people are saying on the subject, which will help you to see your way through to what you want for yourself. So much more is being said than in the past, and by experts; I wonder if most of us have correspondingly increased our ability to listen, and consequently to understand and evaluate. The problem is not one of condemning, but of understanding in your own way, so that you are able to insist on and to achieve the highest possible standards. Sincerely and seriously, to the best of your ability, determine how YOU like whatever you are considering—personally, from the standpoint of function, beauty, basic good design, character, suitability, and practicality. And the keyword to that analysis is *personally*. Your home is, after all, *your* home. See that it is.

SKETCH OF LIVING ROOM, *Illustrating Color Areas*

Traditional

Living room of house in *Georgetown*. Eighteenth-century furniture chosen to go in eighteenth-century room. DECORATOR, *Genevieve Hendricks, A.I.D.*

MET

Italian Baroque chair—carved ornament playful and ornate.

MET

French *fauteuil,* Louis XIV—ornament more restrained.

CU

Italian Rococo open-arm chair—back composed of beautiful combination of free forms

MET

French *fauteuil,* Louis XIV—the frame of this chair is one continuous curve.

FR.

French side chair, Louis XVI—a subtle combination of straight lines and curves.

FR.

French *bergère*, Louis XVI—same as side chair and designed for comfort.

CU

French side chair, Empire—made early in the period of Napoleon.

CU

French side chair, Directoire—neo-classic in feeling.

FR.

French console, Louis XV—enough beautiful free-form curves in this piece to inspire fifty designs.

MET

Italian commode, late eighteenth-century—post-Rococo, shows classic influence.

MET

French commode, Louis XVI—ormolu decoration, marble top.

FR.

French desk, Empire—early and fine, ormolu mounts, marble top.

CU

English side chair, Queen Anne—a beautifully simple one.

MET

English side chair, Chippendale, showing Chinese influence.

MET

English side chair, Hepplewhite—typical shield back, fine design and carving.

MET

English side chair, Sheraton—painted; an elegant and choice.

MET

English open-arm chair, Adam Brothers—perfection of line consistent.

MET

English mirror, Chippendale—shows Rococo and Louis XV influence; he did many different styles.

NEW YORK PUBLIC LIBRARY

English upholstered chair, Victorian—a busy, happy, and comfortable example.

FR.

English Regency secretary—a rare example, rosewood.

MET

Early American chair—ladder-back with rush seat.

MET

American side chair, Georgian—Chippendale design; his most typical type with ball-and-claw foot.

MET

American side chair, Federal—typical design of Duncan Phyfe.

CU

American side chair, Victorian—a fine Belter chair.

MET

American lowboy–style of Chippendale.

MET

American Pembroke table, Georgian–this design popular with Hepplewhite.

MET

American secretary, Georgian–block-front.

MET

American chest of drawers, Federal –eagle feature of ornament.

Your Bird's-Eye View of the Periods

The evolution of period styles as they are commonly recognized and used today is a subject in itself. It is one on which many books have been written, and it has been included, in a fairly comprehensive manner, in several good textbooks on interior decoration. We are not concerned with it in this book. However, for those who are interested in traditional design, I have worked out a brief and condensed description, based on the period styles most frequently used in this country in the past few decades, which will serve as a reference.

It is my opinion that too much has been made of identification in this matter of period styles. It is certainly essential for the individual who makes a study of it, but as an interested housewife, you needn't feel that you must become an authority on it just because you enjoy having some old pieces in your home. And it is ridiculous for you to feel inferior or chagrined if you can't identify all those you like as to time and style. Although a little knowledge can give you an increased pleasure in what you do have, it is much more important for you to know whether or not it is good and will look well in your home. If, on the other hand, you simply want to get a definite idea of the character of any one of the better-known periods, this chapter will provide it. If you are just plain modern-minded and have no interest in the subject, skip it.

There has also been a great deal of emphasis on authenticity and certainly if you want a genuine piece you should be sure that you have it. At the same time, if you like a style and your purpose doesn't require a true period piece, it is possible to buy excellent reproductions. It is also important, here, to know whether you are getting a well-designed piece and to be sure that it will fit into your home. But it certainly isn't necessary to be apologetic if you assemble a nice period room entirely with reproductions. Some of our best decorators do it beautifully and with pride. This kind of furniture is sold through decorators and your decorator can be of help in judging the design as well as its appropriateness for your particular room and purpose.

In addition to this furniture, which is usually machine-made with some hand finishing, there are a few good places where it is being copied exactly from pieces made during the period, and constructed completely by hand. These establishments are found mainly in the eastern part of the country and particularly in New England, where the things that originally came from a special area are reproduced. This kind of construction comes very close to the original, since the old things were made by hand and by artisans who cared and worked lovingly over every turn and joining. They are not inexpensive, but they are good to know about for the person who is interested in having fine workmanship and can't find the right old piece, or has one that is worn out and can't be repaired.

Williamsburg is an example of a fine job of restoring. Some of it is original, but much of it was either gone or too badly deteriorated to use. Sixty-six of the old buildings were repaired or restored and eighty-four reproduced on the original foundations. It has been done with such care, based on knowledge, taste, and feeling for the period, that it is impossible for most people to distinguish between the new and the old. There are other commendable projects that are similar, but none quite as large or complete. It seems such a sound idea to keep some of the old settlements in good condition, not only for their beauty, but because it makes it possible for us actually to feel the continuity of the historical development of our country. They have gone even further in making real the conception of the way of life in those days by the licensing of reproductions—furniture, accessories, fabrics and wallpapers, as well as a series of wall colors. The furniture and accessories are made by craftsmen and all the products included in the licensing are carefully supervised so that there can be no compromising of standards.

While any good reproduction can be an addition to the home of taste and distinction, you must be able to select it with care, and if possible with the help of the person trained to know—the decorator. As is explained in an earlier chapter, no matter where you buy it this will not make it cost more. Today there is, on the market, far too much badly designed furniture that is being promoted and sold as period reproductions—or possibly just period-inspired designs. In any case, presumably someone's notion of work done during the period is back of this merchandise, but it must be far, far back in the dim distance because all of the good qualities seem to be missing. The scale and proportion are bad, the applied decoration tastelessly and clumsily done, and the total effect is a perfect example of bad taste. Furniture of this kind represents the true spirit of the time as little as some African Modern (so labeled) represents the sound and good design of today.

One word has been so consistently misused in furniture merchandising that I suppose there is little use in trying to correct it. But it might help if you knew and perhaps if a lot of us try, we can set it straight. The word is provincial. The name French Provincial has been used to designate a certain eighteenth-century style of furniture made during the time of Louis XV, and this is incorrect. The word is spelled the same in French as it is in English and it means the same and I quote from the dictionary, "of or belonging to the provinces." It is not confined to one style of design, but refers to any furniture made in the country shops or the smaller places and is usually simpler and less sophisticated than the more elegant pieces that came from the cities, where more competition demanded greater variety and refinement.

There are a few styles of the past that have been used in this country, but on the whole, locally, and never to the extent of being generally understood and sold throughout the country. The provincial designs done by the peasants in the Scandinavian countries, Germany, and Austria have had some influence and are fairly well known, but do not constitute a style. The Biedermeier style is somewhat known, as a number of pieces latterly found their way to this country, and in general it was reflected in some of the Victorian furniture. The finishes were mostly wood tones, the beauty of the grain taking the place of painting. It was less classic and less sophisticated than the Empire, with more curves, and not always well made. The ornament was mainly variations of floral motifs, animal and human forms, urns, wreaths, and swags of fruit.

Florida, California, and the Southwest, with their warm climates and history of Spanish explorers, have been influenced by Spain more than the rest of the country. The white or light-colored stucco walls with tile roof, the patios and enclosed gardens are familiar to most of us. Many reproductions of the furniture of this style have been made, both good and bad, and there are still many of the old pieces scattered through fine homes of this type. On the whole, since this assumes a way of living practical only in a fairly warm climate, and most of the southern area east of the Mississippi has its own tradition, it has not been generally used in other parts of the country. In Germany the Baroque idea, which came from the Italians, was developed in a fascinating way and had some influence in this country. German artisans used it magnificently in some of their palaces and delightfully in a number of Bavarian churches. They adapted the designs in a highly skilled manner, cheerfully built the churches, and gave them a happiness and gaiety never before permitted in a place of worship, using clear, clean whites (which they manage to keep clean), bright golds, and all kinds of flesh tones with a variety of soft pinks and blues, done in plaster designs with paint.

To illustrate the periods I am using in my Bird's-Eye, I have chosen photographs because I believe they give you a more accurate idea of the period than a line drawing. The photograph shows a piece that actually existed in its own time and there is no chance of interpretation as there could be in a drawing. The use of a chair for each period makes the evolution, comparisons and contrasts easier to catch. I will also show a few cabinet pieces to further illustrate certain periods.

ITALIAN PERIODS

Baroque and Rococo: Depending on the part of Italy, Baroque begins late sixteenth century or early seventeenth century and Rococo runs through middle of eighteenth century.

Large in scale, opulent and ornate. Combined structural and decorative effects in a fantastic way, with a profusion of exaggerated and flowing curves and scrolls used on a sound foundation. Mostly overdone, with no attempt at restraint. After the Reformation, the Church set out to make churches impressive—lavish, grandiose and original ornament designed for visual and emotional appeal—to attract the people. Domestic interiors equally splendid and ornate—furniture on same grand scale, covered with riotous ornament—designed for show rather than comfort. Lots of painted architecture and much use of plaster, especially for simulated draperies and quantities of cherubs—usually hanging from ceiling. Brilliant colors and marbles, real and simulated, both typical. The Rococo evolved from this. Often used together in same building, so it is impossible to say which dominates the style. Completely abandons sound structural foundation—lighter in scale, charming and colorful. Name derives from French word for rock—*rocaille*. Rocks influence ornament but shell most frequently used motif—with bowknots, ribbons, oval wreaths; endless, flowing subtle curves. Nothing geometric—even circles became slightly oval. Furniture and interiors from Venice especially well known and colorful.

FRENCH PERIODS

Louis XIV: 1643–1715 Partially contemporary with Italian Baroque, from which it gets its start. Strongly influenced by the King—his main ideal magnificence. Large in scale, formal, pompous and elegant. Interior architecture highly decorated, furniture heavy and masculine. Basic straight lines with heavy ornamentation, making use of many geometric curves. Ebony, oak, walnut common woods. Much use of ormolu (gilded bronze) and marquetry (wood inlay), with which was used tortoise shell and German silver. Tapestries often hung on walls (helped, or at least seemed to help, keep rooms warm), usually allegorical subjects. Heavy materials—tapestry, brocades, brocatels, satins and damasks. Chairs began to be a little comfortable and bookcases to be more common—developed from cupboards—as more printed books appeared. Colors strong and fairly dark—deep green, blues, crimson and lots of gold.

Louis XV: 1723–1774 Between 1715 and 1723 France was ruled by a regent and this Regency period (called *Régence* in France and not to be confused with the English Regency) was a transitional one and of interest mainly to specialists. Louis XV style, lighter and smaller in scale, feminine, romantic, gay and whimsical. Also frivolous and sometimes lacking in restraint. No more straight lines. Freehand curves (none geometric) in everything—architecture, furniture, and ornament—that were irregular, light, graceful, and flowing. Also used shell with many other motifs such as lozenge, cartouche, etc. Little that was not based on free form and the freedom was so completely a genuinely natural expression that our free-form designers of today could learn much from it. The style was remarkable in its inventiveness of ornament. Designs based on the delightful antics of monkeys, behaving like human beings, called *singerie* and those making use of and often slightly kidding the Chinese influence, called *Chinoiserie*, have yet to be equaled in originality of concept, and as beautiful and strictly appropriate decorative design. Jean Pillement was a designer who made beautiful use of these themes. Considerable use of wood paneling, both painted and natural. Oak, walnut, cherry, and fruit woods common. Rooms intimate, furniture made to fit the human figure and all of it comfortable. Perfected chaise longue. Leather often used for table tops. Velvets, damasks, satins, and some taffeta used. Colors soft—off-white or gray going toward mauve, green, cream often used with gold.

Louis XVI: 1774–1789 Return to classicism and straight lines, used with controlled curves—soft curves used with straight lines; a chair usually had straight, tapered legs and a straight back, but back could have an oval shape and sides of seat might be curved. Geometric curves used in decoration—much of it carved. Feminine, sentimental, and small in scale. Architecture and design both balanced, orderly, and symmetrical. Carved-wood ornament included garlands, swags, wreaths of flowers, and all kinds of classical designs —encouraged by Pompeian excavations started in 1765. Increase in number of pieces of furniture. Beds smaller with beautiful wood frames showing. Wood paneling and furniture of same woods used during Louis XV—more of it painted. Silks and cottons main fabrics. First use of *toile de Jouy*—printed cotton with symmetrically placed scenes—usually pastoral and often in medallions. Stripes, and small conventional allover patterns popular. Colors were soft, delicate tones of light gray-blues, greeny-gray, pinky-gray, and off-whites suitable to small scale and intimacy of rooms and furnishings.

Directoire: 1789 (Revolution) or 1795 (Directory)–1804 Only style between Louis XVI and the Empire. Same slender forms and straight lines as preceding period, but simpler, with little or no ornament. Severe background with strong Pompeian influence. Some military ornament used—drums, trumpets, spears, stars, Liberty caps, and regular classic motifs. Light, graceful, delicate and simple with good proportion. Light fruit wood, ebony, and mahogany popular woods. Less paint and more wood tones. Colors either bright and fresh—red, white, and blue of French flag popular—or subtle reds, greens, blacks, etc., taken from Pompeian houses.

Empire: 1804–1814 Napoleon not artistic—only concerned with splendor because he needed solid, grand background to help in putting himself and his power across. Strong classic influence. At first simple and severe—gradually became more ornate and eventually overdone. Severity replaced former intimacy and graceful, gay, whimsical feeling. Absolute symmetry combined with symbols of power—inspiration Roman glory and the goal classic accuracy (literal). Egyptian motifs frequently used after that campaign—obelisk became important form. Furniture much less comfortable—much more of it painted—mahogany popular. Wood paneling decorated with painting. Fabric used on walls—either stretched or draped. Wallpaper became popular. Military motifs still in favor such as laurel, victory wreath, torch, and eagle. Also swan and honeysuckle and Napoleon's own symbol, the bee. Bee and rosette often used as central motif and in allover repeat patterns. Color important—bold but subtle—wine reds, grays, deep greens, mustard yellows and gold, blues and royal purples. This period sparked the English Regency, German Biedermeier and was felt both in Italy and our country, where there are slight Empire styles.

ENGLISH PERIODS

Queen Anne: 1702–1714 Not as commonly used in this country as later periods but had strong influence on later design—particularly early Georgian. Marks transition (with William and Mary) from heavy English Renaissance to Georgian. Lighter, with more curves and less straight lines. Beginnings of comfortable furniture—upholstered love seat, beautiful Queen Anne chairs we still use, and refinement and improvement of Windsor chairs. More and greater variety of tables; secretaries replaced huge, heavy chests. Walnut a favorite wood—later some mahogany. Rich and heavy fabrics. Colors influenced by Chinese rugs and porcelains—soft reds, blues, greens, and golds used with off-whites.

Georgian: 1714–1812 Actually more than one period in style and covers three rulers—George I, II, and III. Changed greatly from beginning to end. Several outstanding designers of furniture and interiors—to be described individually. In beginning, much wood paneling in pine and walnut. Interiors large in scale and somewhat formal and grandiose. Architectural detail used lavishly—lion's head a favorite subject. Furniture mostly mahogany. Designs gradually became lighter and more delicate and Pompeian and Greek influence felt. In latter part of period satinwood largely replaced mahogany.

Thomas Chippendale: 1718–1779 Three cabinetmakers named Chippendale—father and son of this Thomas. This one the most famous. Designed and made all kinds of furniture—especially well known for his chairs—of a great variety of design. Went through several phases, mostly in this order: English, French, Chinese, and Gothic. At first fairly heavy in scale, gradually furniture became lighter. Favorite material mahogany. So prolific that some of his pieces aren't good. Did a great variety of wonderful mirrors. (Son carried on his work—quantities of it around.) Published *The Gentleman and Cabinet Maker's Director* in 1754—widely used—helped to popularize his work. Interiors elegant, using rich fabrics with soft but definite colors—yellows, green-grays, and sometimes lacquer red.

Adam Brothers: 1728–1794 Robert Adam most talented and famous of four brothers—all architects who had a powerful influence on design. He died in 1792. They were first to design complete ensembles—included room and everything in it. Not cabinetmakers but had their designs made by others—sometimes Chippendale or Hepplewhite. Inspired by classic excavation—Robert visited those in Dalmatia. Strict in observance of classic design. Architecture decorated with designs done in plaster relief and painted over in soft tones. Furniture also decorated with similar motifs—carved, painted or applied—Wedgwood panels sometimes used. Liked mahogany best but used other woods and gradually more and more satinwood. Did not specialize in chairs—designed all kinds of other pieces—cabinets, bookcases, and sideboards—responsible for popularity of that piece. Furniture mostly had straight, tapering legs, basic rectangular forms used with some relief of a curve in shape of back or seat. Similar in feeling to Louis XVI—contemporary (partly) with it. Their colors part of their trademark—very soft blues, grays, mauves, or yellows—used with white and a certain gray-green that is called "Adam green." Fabrics elegant and in pattern, small in scale.

Thomas Sheraton: 1750–1806 Spent much time on drawing of his designs—published three editions of his book, *The Cabinet-Maker's and Upholsterer's Drawing Book.* Said to have been good at adapting designs of others but did create style of his own. Early work influenced by Adam brothers and Louis XVI. Used straighter lines than Hepplewhite and made more cabinet pieces—especially for dining room and boudoir. Satinwood and cane often used with exceptionally fine inlay, making use of exotic woods such as holly, tulipwood, rosewood, etc. Later work inferior to early things. Liked silk with a floral pattern and stripes and also used printed chintzes, linens, and toiles. Frequently combined a soft blue with white or a light yellow.

George Hepplewhite: unknown–1786 Little known of his life. In 1788 his wife published a book he had written, *The Cabinet Maker's and Upholsterer's Guide.* Style lighter and more delicate than Chippendale's. Specially known for chairs—with straight tapered legs and often a shield-shaped back. Started with mahogany but used more satinwood and decorated it with inlay and painted designs. His aim "to unite elegance with utility" but furniture was sometimes weak due to elegance of design and type of construction. Liked stripes on silks and satins, and conventional designs using such motifs as ribbons and shields. Same soft, pale colors liked by Sheraton were used by him.

English Regency: 1811–1820 Regency actually ended in 1820, but influence of this style lasted until time of Queen Victoria. Following era of great designers, there was a definite decline, started in late eighteenth century and now very apparent. Social background artificial and reflected in design which eventually became superficial. Nothing original—cheerfully copied French. Somewhat severe and inclined to be simple; unfortunately not sufficient concern for proportion. Thomas Hope most important designer of furniture. Paneling practically forgotten—plaster walls, painted dark, with the architecture in light colors. Pilasters and pediments frequently used. Elegant and brilliantly colored fabrics—yellow, dark crimson, purple; in velvets, satins, and damasks. Layers of curtains at the windows. Silhouettes emphasized by strong value contrasts —light green, fawn, terra cotta used with deep greens and rich browns. In spite of its decadence, the period made some contributions and made a practice of designing house, furnishings, and garden as a unit for the first time.

Victorian: 1837–1901 This is a veritable hodgepodge. Because of industrial expansion, everything had to be had in a hurry and machinery sped up production—a steady flow of new things. Speed of execution replaced standards of design: craftsmanship and pride in it no longer an element in the building of furniture. At the same time the Queen's lack of interest in art resulted in a dearth of art leadership—consequently no real style developed. Many influences —Greek, Venetian, and Gothic—strongest the Louis XV period of France. To see the difference, contrast one chair leg of each—one curve is beautiful and subtle and the other exaggerated, mechanical. Everything elaborate, overdone, and confused, although it could have the virtue of a crazy kind of honesty. Quantities of lace, fringe, tassels, and a wide variety of bric-a-brac, from blackamoors (they often had real character) to wax flowers under glass. Everything heavy—wallpapers, woods, and colors—with lots of reds, greens, and gold used.

AMERICAN PERIODS

Early American: 1620–1725 The word Colonial has been used to refer to any kind of furniture made in this country before the nineteenth century, but actually it is correct to use it only for the period ending with the establishment of the United States. Early furniture was simple, unsophisticated, and purely functional—appearance gradually became more important. Houses mostly of wood because of its availability as forests were cleared. Furniture provincial—made of local woods, whatever at hand—pine, oak, and maple most common. In the beginning, if there was any style it was a crude copy of what had been brought from England—or remembered. Regional and in general very individual, depending greatly on where made and by whom. Pennsylvania German good example—still well known. Early crude furniture provided minimum of comfort, convenience, and beauty. Gradually became better and gave way to simple settees, cupboards (corner and hutch type), gate-leg and butterfly tables, four-post beds and a variety of beautiful mirrors, which evolved as they had more time to give to appearance of designs. Stiff ladder-back chairs replaced by more comfortable Windsor, which was developed into a fine piece of furniture. Colors cheerful—soft and grayed reds, yellows, blues, and greens found mainly in simple fabrics.

Georgian: 1725–1780 As necessity for survival and pure function (varied in different parts of country) decreased, much more importance given to design. Still regional differences, but less provincial and a generally consistent development. Houses now made of stone and brick, where available. More trained cabinetmakers—some of them fine craftsmen coming from England. Interiors and furniture became finer and more sophisticated. Designs of Georgian architecture in England and many pieces of furniture of the period brought over with every shipload of immigrants. These were used and adapted to the homes being built here. Stairways in the grand houses especially decorative and elegant. Architectural detail carefully thought out. More comfort in every way. In general, designs followed those in England—a few years later and somewhat simplified. Furniture made with both straight and curved legs and several kinds of feet. Lowboys, highboys, desks of all kinds, canopied beds, tables—tilt-top, piecrust, and pier—clocks of all types and more mirrors. Chippendale, Hepplewhite, and Sheraton designs interpreted in an individual way but definitely recognizable—sometimes copied. Toward end of period, beginning of classic revival. English cotton prints imported. Also had India prints, damasks, and crewel-embroidered fabrics from Europe. Colors soft (like Williamsburg) and some more emphatic ones—red, brown, and green.

Federal: 1789–1825 Revolution temporarily halted trend toward elegance. After end of war, new style developed—mixture of French Empire, English Regency with a native quality. Based on Georgian but finer in scale, simple in design, with a feeling of classicism—a reaction against the somewhat extravagant decoration of some of the Georgian things. Showed evidence of a distinct and purely national influence—represents first years of our republic. Samuel McIntire and Charles Bulfinch outstanding architects who had a strong influence. Duncan Phyfe came from Scotland and produced many good pieces of furniture between 1795 and 1820 under influence of Adam brothers and Sheraton before his work became somewhat heavy and decadent. Style sometimes called American Empire started at this time but never became a real period (basically a combination of Federal with French Empire, although heavier). Eagle a most frequently used motif, done in a very decorative manner (lends itself) and also stars and stripes, leaves, and—particularly in designs by Duncan Phyfe—the lyre. Rather elegant fabrics used and more variety than in any previous period. Olive green in a soft tone, light blues and grays, and occasionally the colors of the flag.

Victorian: 1830–1880 Similar to English period in general characteristics but even more hodgepodge. Gothic trend results in some crazy but interesting houses in various parts of the country. As in England, furniture machine-made with not much chance of true craftsmanship. Ostentation more in demand than quality. Genuine boisterousness endears it to many people today even when they disapprove of the design. John Belter probably best-known individual furniture designer. Many of his things have survived and are on collectors' lists, ornate, but interesting and full of character. Same reds, greens, golds, and heavy wood tones as used in England. Lots of roses and quantities of bric-a-brac.

Defining and Pronouncing Words Used in Decorating

This glossary is intended to be of practical help. It includes words that frequently appear in articles on interior design. Many of them have come to have a familiar sound, but you may be vague as to their specific meaning. To develop understanding and confidence in the use and pronunciation of these words, refer to the glossary. It is by no means comprehensive, in the sense of a complete guide, but should be helpful.

APPLIQUE French word meaning bracket, usually used in the decorating profession to refer to any type of wall lighting fixture. (Pronounced *appleek.*)

APRON A flat piece of wood under and at right angles to table top or chair seat, extending between legs, usually several inches deep, sometimes shaped and slightly recessed.

ARABESQUE A kind of scroll pattern in which leaves, flowers, fruits, and geometrical forms are intertwined. Often used within a panel with lines of design following spiral direction.

ARCADE A line of arches and their supporting columns. Used in support of covered passageways and especially in hot climates over the sidewalk to protect people from the sun. Bologna, Italy, famous for many arcaded streets, and Rue de Rivoli, a well-known street in Paris.

ARCH A curved structure used as a support over an open space. May be geometrical—part of a circle, or higher, or flattened at the top—variety of proportions possible. In masonry, put together with wedge-shaped blocks. The form also used as decoration, either sunken or projecting from wall.

ARMOIRE French word for a closet or wardrobe, usually furnished with a lock. Designed in the eighteenth century as a beautiful piece of furniture. They are customarily used instead of closets, which are not built into French houses or hotels. (Pronounced *armwarr.*)

ASYMMETRICAL Not symmetrical. See *SYMMETRICAL.*

BALUSTER A slender turned column used as a support for a handrail and sometimes as decoration.

BANQUETTE French word for bench; has come to refer mainly to a long one, placed or built against the wall. Commonly used in restaurants. (Pronounced *bankett.*)

BERGÈRE French word for easy chair. Upholstered, with solid back and sides and a decorative wooden frame showing. First commonly used during the reign of Louis XV, when comfort became important in chair design. (Pronounced *bearjare.*)

BIBLIOTHÈQUE Library—room or building—or a bookcase. (Pronounced *bibleeoteck.*)

BOISERIE French word for wainscot or boarding. Used in this country almost entirely to refer to wood paneling—or anything done in wood as part of a wall. The most beautiful ones designed during the late seventeenth and eighteenth centuries. (Pronounced *bwazeree.*)

BOMBÉ Past tense of French verb meaning to bulge or swell. Most commonly used in commodes or lower part of desks, giving them a rounded front. Used more in the Chippendale, Louis XV, and Rococo periods than any other. (Pronounced *bombay.*)

BOUILLOTTE French word for kettle and refers to a certain kind of table lamp—usually with three candles and a round, shallow, metal shade. Table on which it often was used called by the same name, round, with four legs and usually made with a gallery. (Pronounced *bwouyott.*)

BUTTERFLY TABLE Small table with drop leaves, supported by wing brackets in the shape of a butterfly. Commonly used in the American colonies.

CABRIOLE A type of leg that curves inward from the foot and terminates at the top with a reverse curve. A very subtle kind of curve used both in England and France in the eighteenth century. (If you want to learn about curves, try to sketch one.)

CANDELABRUM (pl. candelabra) or *CANDELABRA* (pl. candelabras) A large branched candlestick.

CARTOUCHE French word for cartridge—refers to a scroll-like ornament, often an oval. Frequently used as central motif in a design. (Pronounced *cartoosh.*)

CASEMENT WINDOW A window hinged at one side—usually opens out.

CHAISE LONGUE French expression for a long chair. Became popular and very comfortable during eighteenth century. Often in two pieces, sometimes in three. Intended for a combination of sitting and reclining. (Pronounced *shezz long.*)

CHIMNEY PIECE (see *MANTEL*).

CHINOISERIE French expression for the adaptation of Chinese designs—used to decorate wood panels, wallpapers, textiles, and furniture. See *LOUIS XV.* (Pronounced *sheenwozrie.*)

CLASSIC Refers to design based on the artistic standards, principles, and methods of the ancient Greeks and Romans—balanced, formal, austere, and usually simple and objective.

COMMODE French word for a chest of drawers. Replaced chests which opened from the top; drawers made chests much more convenient—the meaning of the word. (Pronounced *kom'mode.*)

COMPOSITION An arrangement of parts so as to form a harmonious and unified whole. See definition of unity in Chapter 2.

CONSOLE French word for table or bracket. Originally a bracket or shelf fastened to wall. Now includes small tables designed to be used against the wall. (Pronounced *kon'sole.*)

CORNICE Originally the crowning member of an architectural composition. Now usually refers to the horizontal molding which projects along the top wall of a room or building. Used also for concealing curtain fixtures in a way similar to valance.

CREDENZA Or *credence,* French word for sideboard. A cabinet usually combining shelves and doors for storage. Originally intended for dining room but now frequently used in living room, library, or hall.

DADO The lower part of the wall of a room if treated differently from the area above it, usually with an ornamental (architectural) border or paneling.

DORMER WINDOW A window set upright in a sloping roof.

DOUBLE-HUNG WINDOW Commonly used window with two sections—one sliding down from the top, the other up from the bottom.

ELEVATION A flat, scale drawing of the front, side, or rear of a building or piece of furniture. Shows no perspective.

ESCRITOIRE French word for secretary or writing desk. (Pronounced *eskreetwoir.*)

FAÇADE The face or front of a building. (Pronounced *fassodd.*)

FAUTEUIL French word for armchair. An upholstered chair with open space between arm and seats as distinguished from *bergère,* which is solid. (Pronounced *foetoy.*)

FIDDLEBACK The back of a chair in Queen Anne style. Back splat similar in shape to a fiddle.

FINIAL An ornamental terminal in the form of a sort of knob. Can be a plain ball, or pineapple, flame, or foliage, usually ending in somewhat of a point. On a lamp, used on the top of screw that holds shade.

FIREBACK An iron lining for the back of the fireplace. Often beautifully decorated. Intended to protect masonry and reflect heat.

FLOCK PAPER Wallpaper with a raised pattern, made of powdered wool, which has a soft, rather fuzzy surface.

GALLERY A raised rim of wood or metal—often a railing in miniature. Used on the edge of a piece of furniture.

GIMP A flat, narrow, braidlike trim used as a finish on upholstered furniture and curtains.

GIRANDOLE Comes from Italian word *girandola* meaning a wheel-like cluster of fireworks. A candelabra with arms, often ornamented and usually forms a circle of lights.

GRISAILLE A style of painting using only values of one color —usually gray or soft, grayed browns. Often intended to give the effect of plaster relief. (Pronounced *grizzeye.*)

HIGHBOY A tall chest of drawers mounted on legs as an important part of the design.

HUTCH A cabinet dating from seventeenth-century England, with doors. Designed for storage and usually made of oak.

INLAY Form of decoration made by setting pieces of wood, metal, etc., in a surface to make a design which is level with the surface when finished.

KNEEHOLE DESK A flat-top desk with drawers at either side and open space in the center for the knees.

LADDER-BACK A type of chair back which uses horizontal slats between the uprights, similar to a ladder.

LOGGIA An arcaded and roofed gallery built into or projecting from the side of a building.

LOVE SEAT Any small upholstered sofa—usually between four and five feet in length.

LOWBOY A small table with drawers, used as a wall piece. Often the same as the lower part of a highboy.

LOZENGE Diamond-shaped motif frequently used in decorative ornament.

MANTEL The complete facing around the opening of a fireplace, including any shelf used above it. Also called chimney piece.

MARQUETRY From French word meaning inlaying or patchwork. A special kind of inlay used in fine veneer surfaces. (Pronounced *mocketry*).

MEDALLION A round or oval design, sometimes in relief, and usually containing a portrait of some kind, or an ornamental motif.

MILLEFLEURS French, meaning a thousand flowers. Used to describe small allover background with pattern made from leaves and flowers. Found in many of the fifteenth-century tapestries. Shows incredible ingenuity, charm, and originality. (Pronounced *meelflewr.*)

MITER or *MITRE* A kind of joint formed by fitting two pieces (usually wood) together that have been beveled to the same angle —usually 45 degrees. Illustrated by corners of a door trim or a picture frame.

MOTIF French word for theme. A central or repeated figure in a design. (Pronounced *moteef.*)

MOUNTS Ornamental metalwork applied to furniture—usually cabinet pieces, less often chairs. Empire period went in heavily for mounts.

NEOCLASSIC Refers to a revival of the classic style and form. History records several such revivals.

NICHE A recessed space in a wall, usually planned to show some kind of a statue or ornamental object. Often classic in design. (Pronounced *neesh* or *nitch.*)

ORMOLU In French *or moulu* meaning ground gold. A kind of gilded bronze used extensively for decoration of furniture, especially under the reign of Louis XIV. Handsome designs made which were cast in bronze. (Pronounced *ormoloo.*)

OTTOMAN A comfortable backless, cushioned seat: used, with a chair, as a footrest.

PANEL A surface—usually on wall or ceiling, set off from the surrounding surface by being raised, recessed, or framed.

PARQUET French word for flooring or inlaid work. Refers to flooring that makes use of the strips of wood in a geometric pattern. Parquet de Versailles and herringbone two well-known patterns. (Pronounced *parquay.*)

PEDIMENT Originally a low-pitched, triangular gable on roof at exterior ends of a Greek temple. Has come to mean any similar form used in decoration of doorway, over mantel, furniture, etc.

PEMBROKE TABLE Rectangular tables, usually small with drop leaves that may be rounded or squared. Often made of mahogany or satinwood, with square, tapered legs and a drawer. Hepplewhite fond of this design.

PERSPECTIVE Means of showing a solid object on a surface so as to make it appear to have a third dimension. Must adjust sizes involving distance and depth, to make them convincing to the eye.

PIECRUST TABLE A small table, often round, with an edge

that is raised and scalloped or fluted. Frequently used on tilt-top tables.

PILASTER A flat, rectangular feature, using the design of a column but projecting only a few inches from the wall. Used commonly in any neoclassic design.

PLAN A drawing or diagram showing the arrangement in horizontal section of a structure or a piece of furniture. What you would see if it were possible to slice it through just above the bottom.

PLINTH A projecting piece at the base of a vertical—column, pedestal, door trim, or any similar architectural part.

REFECTORY Originally the dining hall in a monastery or convent. Usually used now to describe a long narrow table of a design similar to those used in such dining halls.

REPOUSSÉ From French word meaning to push away. Refers to relief work on thin metal that is formed by beating it from the underside. (Pronounced *repoosay.*)

REPRODUCTION A copy that is a close imitation or duplication of an original. Usually involves working with designs of an earlier time.

RESTORATION The restoring or putting back into normal condition of anything that has been damaged from use or age—or both.

SINGERIE French word for monkey trick. Refers to whimsical and elaborate designs based on the antics of monkeys in human poses. (Pronounced *sanjaree.*)

STRETCHER Name given to wooden brace used between legs of furniture. May be flat, round, or shaped.

SWAG A decorative motif using a festoon of leaves, flowers, or fruit; or fabric, draped. Many variations and frequently used as design for carving.

SYMMETRICAL In a design, equal division of form, size, and arrangement of parts—identical halves.

TAMBOUR From the French word for drum. Usually refers to small slats of wood fastened to a flexible backing, so they can be pulled back and forth over an opening.

TESTER The canopy on a four-post bed.

TILT-TOP TABLE A table with a hinged top so that it may be used upright.

TOILE DE JOUY French for cloth of Jouy. Refers to cottons printed at Jouy. (Pronounced *twoll de jooey.*)

TOLE Painted and decorated tin. (Pronounced *toll.*)

TORCHÈRE French word for candelabra. Often large, standing on the floor. (Pronounced *torshere.*)

VALANCE Usually made of fabric or wood, shaped and hung horizontally over draperies—at windows, on beds, etc.

VENEER A very thin layer of wood, usually fine grain, bonded to a heavier piece. Veneered furniture is considered by many to be inferior to pieces made of solid woods. This is true only in cheap, badly made pieces. The finest pieces in the earlier days were veneered because only by using veneer were the designers able to control the grain as part of the design. Their craftsmanship in putting the veneer together was of a superb kind and this is also well done in fine pieces today.

Description of Color Names

Alizarin Crimson—strong, pure red
Burnt Sienna—warm, reddish brown
Burnt Umber—rich, live, and warm brown—less gray than Van Dyke
Cadmium Orange—yellow orange
Cadmium Red—yellow red—goes toward orange
Cadmium Yellow—Deep, goes slightly toward orange
Medium, stronger and deeper than lemon
Light, goes toward lemon yellow
Carmine—strong red, slightly bluer than Alizarin
Cerulean Blue—light, sharp peacocky blue
Charcoal Gray—dark, warm gray
Chrome Yellow—Deep, goes toward orange
Medium, strong color—less orange, more lemon
Pale, lighter, goes toward lemon
Chromium Oxide—good, clear green—slightly yellow
Cobalt Blue—basic blue—intense sky color
Crimson Lake—strong red, between Alizarin and Carmine
Emerald Green—light, bright green
Gamboge—strong, clear yellow
Geranium Lake—bright red, slightly pinker than Alizarin

Hooker's Green—good, strong green—sometimes numbered 1 and 2. Two is darker
Indian Red—brownish or tawny red
Indigo—deep, dark, strong blue
Lemon Yellow—color of a lemon
Light Red—lighter and more yellow than Indian Red—sometimes called English Red
Mauve—describes a variety of tones—soft, with a purplish cast
Neutral Tint—deep gray, with a slight purplish cast
New Blue—strong, clear blue—between Cobalt and Ultramarine
Olive Green—grayed yellow green similar to a green olive
Payne's Gray—deep gray with a bluish cast
Prussian Blue—sharp, strong, and deep blue
Raw Sienna—brownish yellow
Raw Umber—deeper and browner than Raw Sienna
Sap Green—yellow green—not very bright
Scarlet Lake—sharp, bright red—goes toward orange
Sepia—very dark, grayed brown
Ultramarine—strong, clear blue, slightly darker than Cobalt
Van Dyke Brown—good, clear, strong brown
Vermilion—strong, clear yellow red—sometimes called Chinese Red
Viridian—sharp, bright, blue green
Yellow Ochre—light, slightly brownish yellow—lighter than Raw Sienna

Index